Series / Number 90-006

# A Paradigm for the Comparative Analysis of Legislative Systems

**JOHN G. GRUMM**

*Wesleyan University*

SAGE PUBLICATIONS / Beverly Hills / London

*For information address:*

SAGE PUBLICATIONS, INC.
275 South Beverly Drive
Beverly Hills, California 90212

SAGE PUBLICATIONS, INC.
St George's House / 44 Hatton Garden
London EC1N 8ER

International Standard Book Number 0-8039-0364-2

Library of Congress Catalog No. L.C. 73-92220

FIRST PRINTING

*C I*    JAN. 2 2 1979

When citing a professional paper, please use the proper form. Remember to cite the
correct Sage Professional Paper series title and include the paper number. One of the
two following formats can be adapted (depending on the style manual used):

(1) KORNBERG, A. et al. (1973) "Legislatures and Societal Change: The Case of
Canada." Sage Research Papers in the Social Sciences (Comparative Legislative
Studies Series, No. 90-002). Beverly Hills and London: Sage Pubns.

*OR*

(2) Kornberg. Allan et al. 1973. *Legislatures and Societal Change: The Case of
Canada.* Sage Research Papers in the Social Sciences, vol. 1, series no. 90-002
(Comparative Legislative Studies Series). Beverly Hills and London: Sage Publications.

# Contents

This is one of the first group of research papers in the Comparative Legislative Studies Series, being published by Sage Publications in cooperation with the Consortium for Comparative Legislative Studies. The purpose of this series is to make possible the prompt publication and wide distribution of legislative research that has a comparative perspective. The series will include cross-national research on legislative systems, institutions, behavior, and outputs, as well as legislative research in a single nation that tests and develops hypotheses which are significant for comparative research.

In this study, Professor Grumm is seeking to develop a model of the legislative system that will enhance the comparative study of legislatures. Unlike some recent students, he focuses attention on the legislative or lawmaking function, "the formulation and adoption of general rules and policies determining the authoritative allocation of values for society." He is interested in developing a method for measuring the performance of the legislative system, with particular emphasis on its capacity to be responsive to the needs that arise in a society. The model that he develops is a complex one, but it is one that can be tested empirically. It takes into account political factors that affect legislative performance, and it is particularly sensitive to the problem of time lags in response to needs.

Grumm tests the model by using data from the American states, and demonstrates both the utility of his model and the problems associated with it. Students interested in cross-national research should find this study valuable for their own research, both because it offers a model that they can replicate and because it sheds light on a number of the problems they are likely to encounter in studying legislative performance in any country.

—*MALCOLM E. JEWELL*

# A PARADIGM FOR THE COMPARATIVE ANALYSIS OF LEGISLATIVE SYSTEMS

JOHN G. GRUMM

Wesleyan University

## Introduction

Theoretic development in the field of comparative politics has proceeded at a rapid pace during the past two decades. At least, it seems as though the analyst has a rich variety of competing frameworks or models from which to choose when embarking on research in this field. Among others, there are the structural-functional approach, systems analysis, rationalistic models, and developmental theories. Still, this very richness may be confusing and unsettling. Can the empirical researcher laboring in the field of comparative legislative systems, for example, relate his work to any of this theoretic development? If he tries to, he may discover that the abstractness of the concepts involved obscures any possible reference to empirical reality and be thrown back on his own resources to devise some sort of framework to guide his research. As Holt and Richardson (1970: 70) have put it, most of these approaches have very little deductive power, which is to say they do not contain sets of propositions from which one can readily deduce in a logical manner a wide range of additional propositions that can be empirically verified. Basically, the problem is that we are suffering from the poverty and under-development of empirical theory as such, although we may be embarrassed by the riches found in the more abstract theories.

Certainly it would be foolish to ignore these riches, for, in fact, they can be well used to underwrite the development of a more empirically oriented theory. Let us examine several and learn what might be appropriated from them to support such a project.

*AUTHOR'S NOTE: The author wishes to express his gratitude to the Consortium for Comparative Political Studies for its financial support of the research presented here and to its director, Professor Allan Kornberg, who in a very great measure facilitated, encouraged, and assisted these endeavors. Appreciation is also acknowledged for support from the late Committee on Governmental and Legal Processes of the Social Science Research Council which helped collect many of the data used in this project, and to Wesleyan University for the liberal use of its computer and other facilities.*

To begin with, systems theory would seem to be helpful in structuring our thinking about the legislative system and the interrelations within it. And from Easton's (1965) formulation, it also provides us with a convenient vocabulary for discussing aspects of the political system in general, the forces impinging upon it, and the products of its processes. By itself, it does not seem to be very productive of testable hypotheses, nor does it give us many clues as to what kinds of data we should be collecting and analyzing, but it still should be usable as a framework for an empirical theory that is more deductively fertile.

The structural-functional approach is also valuable in helping us to gain new knowledge of the political system, but it also fails to supply much stimulation for hypothesis production. This approach urges us to focus our attention on structures and functions and warns us to keep them analytically separated. It can and has helped political scientists overcome a tendency to identify certain structures with certain functions automatically. The structural-functionalists have insisted that a given function may be performed by different structures in different political systems and that structures that appear to be similar may perform quite divergent functions in different systems. Analysis based on this approach seeks to explain why one structure rather than another contributes to the satisfaction of a particular function or functions in a particular social system at a given time and then seeks to predict what specific structure or structures will contribute to the satisfaction of a given function at some specific time (Holt, 1967). Nevertheless, this approach only provides a framework within which hypotheses may be generated and to which we will have to add a more articulated theory of the interconnections between structure and function to provide the substance for such hypotheses.

The rationalistic approach, borrowed principally from economics and applied to the study of politics by Riker (1962), Downs (1967), and Tullock (1965), provides a more fertile soil for deductive statements than those mentioned previously. The application of rationalistic models might prove rather helpful in formulating predictive statements about behavior in the legislative process, particularly in regard to coalition formation and in decisions on the allocation of material and financial resources. Of course, the assumptions of rationalism have often been attacked (see especially Simon, 1957: 80-81), and one must concede that there is less rational behavior in political life than there is in the economic marketplace, but testable hypotheses have emanated from this approach, and by testing these we may at least gain some insights into where rationalism is warranted. Furthermore, added benefits of this approach are the rather elegant mathematical formulations used both inductively and deductively which can be adapted to other approaches without accepting the whole package of rationalism with them. Elsewhere I have shown the usefulness of comparative legislative analysis of some of the inductive techniques used in testing rational economic models (Grumm, 1973), and some of these were also found useful in the analysis presented here.

Finally, the developmental approach has been very much in evidence during the past decade or more. There is considerably more substance to it than to systems analysis, and it comes closer to an empirical theory than merely a framework for analysis. Probably the most important methodological contribution of this approach stems from the theory of change incorporated in it. Whereas some of the frameworks mentioned above imply homeostasis and assume stable structures, the developmental approach conceives of structures and functions, as well as environmental factors, as dynamic elements capable of being in a continuous state of change. Although other approaches would not deny the possibility of change, the developmental approach focuses on these changes and concentrates its theoretical concerns on how change takes place within the system. It is important for present purposes because it suggests that legislative structures may be conceived as variables that vary through time as well as cross-nationally and also provides the basis from which some hypotheses may be deduced about the causes and consequences of structural changes. In addition, some of the categories employed in the developmental literature are suggestive of useful ways of perceiving aspects of the legislative system. This is not to say that the developmental approach is the answer to all of the prayers of the comparative legislative analyst. It can certainly be criticized for a number of invalid assumptions, for an element of cultural bias, and for a great deal of conceptual ambiguity. Still, the comparative study of legislatures can profitably borrow much from it.

## TOWARD A COMPARATIVE THEORY OF LEGISLATIVE SYSTEMS

We turn now to more specific considerations of what will be useful to borrow from some of the aforementioned approaches in order to put together a theory for the comparative study of legislative systems. From systems theory we will take the concepts of an interrelated system and subsystem, with definable boundaries and an interactive environment outside the system, and the notion of boundary exchanges between systems, subsystems, and the environment. But we would stop with this because systems theory, in itself, is too "structural" in its implications. It would suggest, for example, that the legislative subsystem was defined by the institutional roles of those included in the legislative structure, that is, what was known as the "legislature." It seems that, under this conception, what is part of the system and what is not is structurally determined.

Structural-functionalism, however, should cause us to question and help us to determine whether the "legislature" actually is doing the legislating for the political system. Borrowing from this approach, we would begin by positing a legislative function as essential to the political system and then determine what structures performed this function and what factors determined which structures would perform it.

Loewenberg has pointed out that a major difficulty with this approach is that one must first of all identify those functions that are both necessary and sufficient for the persistence of certain measurable traits of the system (1972: 10). He asserts, "As long as the legislative function . . . cannot be shown to be both necessary and sufficient for the persistence of any system characteristic, neither its presence nor its absence can have demonstrable consequences for the system." His assertion may well be true; at this point we cannot reliably demonstrate the efficacy of the legislative function. Nevertheless, such considerations should not serve to stifle theoretic development. We have to start somewhere, and it is hardly unreasonable to begin with the assumption that a legislative function is necessary to the persistence of important traits of the political system (it is not clear why this must also be a sufficient cause). I suggest we can proceed by formulating a theory based on the assumption of the significance of the legislative function for certain aspects of the political system; and if this fails to eventuate in a set of predictive statements about behavior within the system, we ought to begin to question the assumption. Furthermore, we would be standing on rather firm ground by assuming that the legislative function had important consequences for the political system. It is hardly a whimsical notion. One may be able to conceive of a political system wherein the legislative function is nonexistent, where there is no structure within the system that performs such a function. But it is so salient a feature of all political systems, at least since the rise of the nation-state, that most students of politics would regard it as an essential feature. This is not to say that all political systems have bodies designated as "legislature," and it may be that, in some instances, this function is performed by a single individual or a small group. But, nevertheless, it is a function that appears to be always performed by some individual or structure and one that must have some important consequences for the rest of the system.

What is meant here by a "legislative function"? This is simply the formulation and adoption of general rules and policies determining the authoritative allocation of values for society. Presumably it can be agreed that the general function of the political system is the authoritative allocation of values, but some might contend it is not absolutely necessary that this allocation be determined by general rules or policies. It is conceivable that it could be entirely arbitrary or random. In fact, random policy determination seems to be a characteristic of totalitarian regimes, which apparently use arbitrariness of political action as a technique of terror. One can also cite examples of Latin-American and African political systems where the enactments of the constitutionally designated legislative body are routinely disregarded by the executive, who acts according to his own policies. But in response to this, one might assert that there are policies and general rules implicit in the actions of even what seem to be arbitrary dictatorial regimes.

If this assertion appears to be stretching the conception of legislative function a bit too far, let us view this function as something that can be measured on a continuum rather than as something having a dichotomized character. We would assume, therefore, that the function would be performed, even if only in a very minor degree, in every political system. One could imagine also a number of dimensions in which the function might be measured. An obvious one would be the degree to which it was institutionalized. The Nazi regime would undoubtedly occupy a position at the lowest end of that continuum and, presumably, the U.S. Congress would occupy a position near the high end. Other dimensions of the legislative function would be the degree of representativeness involved in the performance of the function, the extent of democratic control, the degree of specificity with which the function was performed, and the extent to which it was relatively more latent or manifest. This position therefore asserts that there is a legislative function inherent in all political systems, although in some it may be relatively noninstitutionalized, performed in an authoritarian and unrepresentative manner, relatively nonspecific, and more latent than manifest.

As to the legislative system itself, this can be defined as a system of structures and roles involved in the performance of the legislative function. According to this, the system boundaries are determined by the function of law making. Whatever institutions, structures, roles are involved in that function, these are included within the system. Typically, in polities where there is a body known as "the legislature," it would be included to the extent of its law-making role, but it is conceivable that it may not have such a role and, hence, would not be included.

The advantage of this functional focus for comparative research is that is provides a less ambiguous criterion for determining the objects of our attention than is provided by a structural focus. It should be possible to identify the law-making function in any system, and then the structures and roles involved in its performance. Although the boundaries of a structure may be more easily identifiable than those of a function, the fact remains that is becomes very difficult to formulate a nonfunctional, structural definition of the legislative system that is applicable to all political systems. To be universal, the definition would have to be extremely broad, but a broader definition could risk a breakdown of the comparative process since it could involve the comparison of wholly dissimilar objects.

The term "legislative system" has been used extensively by students of American political behavior, although it has not been used with quite the same meaning as proposed here. Wahlke et al., in a book entitled *The Legislative System* (1962), conceived of it as a system of roles in which the boundaries were defined both institutionally and functionally. That is, they began by selecting their actors exclusively from the legislature and then from that point they were concerned essentially with their roles as legislators or rule-makers. Their analysis did not include all roles that would be involved in the legislative system. On the other hand, Jewell and Patterson (1973: 4-6) included within their conception of the legislative system interest groups, the chief executive, the judiciary, and the bureaucracy. But, they tell us, these individuals and groups are only to be included when they actually interact with the legislature, which is the center of focus for the legislative system. Furthermore, they ascribe a larger number of other functions to the system than to rule making. It is certainly correct to include these other individuals and agencies within the legislative system, but I would not agree on the reasons for including them. The bureaucracy, for example, would not necessarily become part of the legislative system when it reacted with the legislative body unless the nature of that reaction was such that it affected the rule-making function. On this basis, therefore, we might exclude such operations as legislative confirmation of appointments in the executive branch or legislative investigations involving the bureaucracy that were not pointed toward any statutory or policy changes. In taking a functionalist approach, however, we would include in the legislative system some bureaucratic operations that did not involve legislative interaction but which did involve the enactment of policies or the adoption of rules. It is undoubtedly true that the bureaucracies in all countries engage in a self-contained process of policy and rule making and that this proceeds without any reference to a legislative body. This is formalized in the American system through the institution of the independent regulatory commission. Informally, policy making takes place in every branch and department of the federal government, and it differs very little in scope and generality from policies formally enacted by the legislature. Thus, I would include within the bounds of the legislative system any individual, group, or agency whose role involved the formulation and enactment of public policy that determined the authoritative allocation of values, and I would exclude from the system behavior that was not connected to such a role, even where this involved the behavior of so-called legislators.

The tendency for students of American politics to place legislative aseemblies at the center of the legislative system is understandable and even appropriate, probably, in the American context. The constitutional separation of powers and the autonomy, legitimacy, and saleincy of these assemblies have caused these institutions to become of considerable interest to the student of politics. There is no denying the usefulness of studying these institutions as such in the United States and in many foreign political systems; but the institutional analysis of elected assemblies outside the Western world often becomes an exercise in triviality.

Our next concern will be to explore the possibilities of an independent measure of system performance. In defining the legislative system, we have borrowed from the political systems framework and from structural-functional analysis. Now we turn to the study of political development to see what we can take from it.

## THE CONCEPT OF SYSTEM PERFORMANCE

One may analyze legislative behavior and structural characteristics and seek explanations for these without any notion of their ultimate consequences or purposes, but if legislative studies are to have any real coherence and unity, or even utility, they need to be informed by some evaluative conceptions that will permit an assessment of whether the system is performing poorly or well and what features of the system contribute to or subtract from that performance. We need some kind of ultimate "dependent variable" that will serve as a guide in selecting and evaluating independent variables.

Because it has proved difficult to get any consensus on evaluative criteria, some have resorted to the proposition that the survival or stability of a system provides a reasonably good indicator that the system is performing its functions well. This notion seems to be implicit in Easton's political system, and this is probably true of all models based on an organismic analogy. It may be that the mere fact of survival indicates that the system is performing its functions at least at some minimum level of capability, but it does not tell us anything beyond this. Among the systems that have survived, we can conceive that there would be represented a vast range of performance capabilities. Presumably those that did not survive did not perform so well as those that did, but still we are not sure this is true. Random factors outside the system could cause its demise as well as an internal dysfunctioning of the system. Or a poorly functioning system might continue to survive because of the benign environment in which it exists.

A more promising measure of system performance might be the

degree of political development or institutionalization of the political system. It is a compelling notion that the better-developed, more modernized, better-articulated, and, therefore, more institutionalized political systems would be more adaptable and more capable, and would generally perform better according to most criteria. In Huntington's (1968) formulation, institutionalization refers to "the process by which organizations and procedures acquire value and stability." The level of institutionalization of any structure is measured by its adaptability, its structural complexity, its autonomy, and its coherence (1969: 18-22). Thus, the connotation is that institutionalized systems are more stable and adaptable. Three difficulties associated with this connotation should be mentioned, however. One is that stability and adaptability, for reasons noted above, ought not to be regarded as ultimate criteria for assessing the performance of political systems. These systems should do something more than merely survive. Another difficulty is that, even if we want to accept these as some kind of measures of performance, we cannot really be sure that structural complexity, autonomy, and coherence always promote adaptability and stability. To include adaptability among the measures of the level of institutionalization, as Huntington does, is to beg that question. It is still, however, a question we could ask if it were possible to measure adaptability. This leads to the third difficulty—how to measure it. Huntington's solution is not very helpful in that he proposes that we go back to the notion of survival, contending that the age of a structure will be an indicator of its adaptability because anything that has survived for a long time is obviously fairly adaptable. But this is not an altogether valid standard, not only because there are many chance factors that can affect survival, but also because advancing age, instead of producing better adaptability, may lead to rigidities and inflexibilities through structural ossification. We may discover that there is a life cycle of political systems and that, while they may have a high infant mortality rate as a class of organisms, they do also die of old age. Until we know more about these interrelationships, it does not appear that we ought to accept age as a valid measure of adaptability.

The other three measures of institutionalization that Huntington presents could not be regarded as any kind of evaluative criteria but are merely descriptive characteristics of structures. It should be useful at this point, however, to examine these briefly in order to elucidate the concept of institutionalization, which has so many important implications for analysis of legislative systems. Structural complexity involves the multiplication of organizational subunits, either on a hierarchical or functional basis, and the differentiation of separate types of organizational subunits. Polsby (1968) expanded on this notion in his analysis of institutionalization of the U.S. House of Representatives by further defining it in terms of functional specificity, widely shared performance expectations, regularized recruitment to roles, and regularized patterns of movement from role to role. Clearly, structural complexity is rather basic to institutionalization as customarily conceived and would generally be regarded as the most critical indicator of this concept. Autonomy might also be generally accepted as a valid measure of institutionalization and in this context to the extent to which the political organizations and procedures are independent of other social groupings and methods of behavior. Thus, we would not regard a legislature whose procedures and organizational structure were dictated by authority outside this body as an institutionalized structure. Polsby (1968), for example, considers the U.S. House of Representatives to be a highly institutionalized body because its control over committees in terms of procedures and structure and the selection and recruitment of leadership is completely internalized. The other measure is that of coherence, which involves the extent of consensus on the functional boundaries of the group and on the procedures for resolving disputes which come up within these boundaries. Such a measure may not be quite as central to the concept of institutionalization as the others, although it probably is necessary for a certain level of such consensus to exist before any advanced degree of institutionalization is possible.

Huntington has provided us with some attractive measures of institutionalization, but there is considerable controversy still over the definition of this concept and how to measure its dimensions. Richard Sisson (1973: 22), for one, has pointed to the "conceptual tension" implicit in this set of indices. He suggests, for example, that complexity may be disruptive of coherence; autonomy, in terms of pluralization of social representation, may also endanger coherence; and complexity may, in certain instances, be disruptive of autonomy. These variables, therefore, do not proceed to form a syndrome of institutionalization; that is, they do not necessarily seem to "go together." Furthermore, it was noted that, except for "adaptability," these are essentially indices of structure rather than of performance. Thus, it is not altogether clear whether Huntington conceived institutionalization to be a structural or a performance concept.

Eisenstadt (1964) also sought to define institutionalization. While his criteria for measuring it were essentially structural, his definition contained a purposive component. He defined the process of institutionalization as the "organization of a societally prescribed system of differentiated behavior oriented to the solution of certain problems inherent in a major area of social life" (1964: 235-236). Here we have the notion—though admittedly rather vague—of an institutional function that goes beyond mere survival or adaptability. If we could define the "certain problems" that Eisenstadt mentions, then we could see how well the political system was doing in solving these problems. Eisenstadt does not explicitly assert that we can measure institutionalization by measuring its capability in solving social problems—only that an orientation toward such problem solving is an attribute of an institutionalized system. This should not stop us, however, from considering problem-solving capability as a measure of institutionalization; if it did, we might regard institutionalization as the ultimate dependent variable for which we have been looking. But let us not take this route, for there are good reasons, as we shall see, for keeping institutionalization and system performance as separate concepts. Eisenstadt has provided us with a hint of how we might measure performance, but we will be best served by a structural conception of institutionalization closer to Huntington's.

Some of the concepts involved in the developmental literature should prove useful in constructing an empirical theory of the legislative system, but it would be a mistake to regard political development, or institutionalization, or modernization, or stability as ends in themselves. The goal for which political institutions exist is not to become modernized or to become stable but to confront successfully the problems of society.

Possibly, institutionalization contributes to this success, but that must remain a hypothetical matter for the moment. Our ultimate dependent variable has to be a measure of how well the system performs in achieving this goal.

In a broad, theoretical sense, the solution of social problems has always been an end of the state, although the modern state is undoubtedly better equipped, has more resources, and is more committed to deal with them and to deal with them more rationally. But even before Plato there was a recognition that states existed to deal with problems arising from people living together in societies. Such societies could not be automatically self-regulating; so order had to be imposed and justice meted out. The problems of order and justice are still the most basic ones the modern state must confront. But it is true that new problems have arisen in the modern political system, and the meanings of order and justice have changed somewhat. Let us consider the empirical question of what meaning these normative matters have in the modern state.

One would like to know what the aspirations, goals, and strivings were of people from all varieties of cultural backgrounds throughout the world and to be able to generalize about these across cultural backgrounds. This would be helpful in formulating a modern conceptualization of justice. We cannot make a survey in every country, but we can refer to some of the vast literature in comparative political development that has emerged in the past 15 years. A convenient source would be the Committee on Comparative Politics of the Social Science Research Council, which is responsible for the publication of seven volumes of *Studies of Political Development.* The committee's spokesmen, believing they have amassed a sufficient amount of evidence, have been willing to assert that the "imperatives of equality" are the dominant factor pervading all aspects of modern political life and culture and all forms of modern political ideology (Binder et al., 1971: 73-100). The components of this are (1) national citizenship, (2) a universalistic legal order, and (3) achievement norms. Citizenship connotes that aspect of equality derived from one's full membership in a national community and embodied in equal formal rights possessed by all citizens. As this concept has evolved, citizenship has meant membership by all of those incorporated within the nation-state, not just a privileged segment, and has meant that citizens are equally and legitimately concerned with the input or participation function, as well as with the output or distribution function. The notion applies to both liberal-democratic and totalitarian systems in that it embodies the notion of a constant improvement in the social and material welfare of all citizens through technological and social innovation fostered by the political system. The fact that universalistic norms are more prevalent than particularistic ones in a government's relations with its citizenry is closely tied to the realization of equal rights of citizenship. These norms dictate equality before the law, which not only means equality of treatment in the application and adjudication of the law but also the equal right to defend and assert all other rights. The predominance of achievement over ascriptive norms in the allocation of political and bureaucratic roles and the fostering of a socioeconomic system which recognizes the former is the third major component of modern egalitarianism. The emphasis is generally on equality of initial opportunity, and here the right to education is crucial in modern society because allocation of the most valued roles in the stratification system increasingly depends upon educational achievement.

The concept of order also has been given a new dimension in the modern world. It is viewed, not as an end in itself, but as a means of ensuring a maximum degree of security in a very broad sense to the citizens of the polity. Traditionally, security has meant protection against physical or material harm inflicted by one's fellow citizens and against an attack on the nation itself from abroad. Today we add to this protection the notion of "social" security, which is really a protection against deleterious effects of the workings of the social and economic system, and so, very closely connected with the imperatives of equality as well. Furthermore, we might also add that the modern meaning includes security against the arbitrary action of the law enforcer, as well as that of the law breaker. Finally, security now also means the promotion of economic development by the state, which presumably could add to the average individual's economic security and may also be regarded as basic to a strong national defense.

Clearly, this is neither a comprehensive nor an adequate treatment of the ends of the modern state, but for present purposes it should suffice. From this we should be able to deduce what kinds of things the political system ought to be doing and to determine whether or not any specific system is doing any or all of these things well.

Although we have been discussing the ends of the total political system, our concern is still with the legislative subsystem. If one is interested in assessing the performance of the latter, however, he must know the purpose of the former, since the function and purpose of any subsystem are defined by the overall system of which they are a part. The legislative system performs a function for the political system as a whole, and we understand this term "function" to mean the mode of action by which an object fulfills its purpose. The term, therefore, defines an activity and implies a purpose. The activity is the passing of legislation, that is, formulating and enacting general policy. The purpose is to serve the general ends of the political system, which is to confront and solve or ameliorate the problems of society. To determine how well the legislative system is performing, therefore, one needs to analyze the end product of its activity—the policy output—and see how well this contributes to the ends of the total political system.

## A MODEL OF THE POLITICAL SYSTEM

The next stage in the construction of an empirical theory is to develop a model of the political system which will be used as the basis for a more specialized model of the legislative system.

In the long run, the ultimate assessment of a system's performance would have to be based on two factors, its capacity to confront social problems as they emerge and its stability as a system over time. The latter is a necessary consideration in that it affects the reliability of the system's capacity, but, as indicated above, it would not be regarded as an end of the system. Figure 1 is a graphic presentation of the relationships among these factors and those that are causally prior to them.

The final, dependent variable in the system is shown to be goal achievement potential. The overall performance of the system is, in principle, measured by this variable. Alternatively, we might have labeled this "problem-solving potential," but this has a rather short-run implication to it. "Goal achievement" has a broader, more inclusive connotation and is meant to reflect the capacity as well as the reliability dimension. Opera-

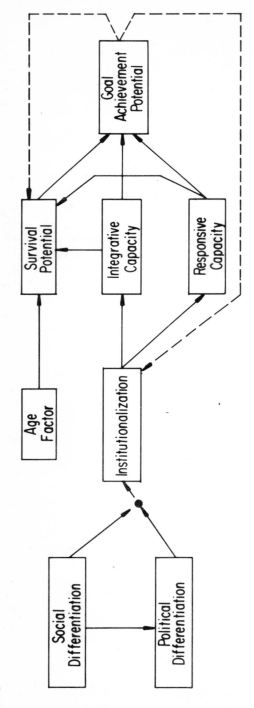

Figure 1. MODEL OF GOAL – ORIENTED POLITICAL SYSTEM

tionally, as is explained below, goal achievement potential measures the rate at which the system is approaching its goals.

Working back through the system, one will note that the term survival potential is used instead of stability. This is because stability, per se, cannot logically be considered a cause of goal achievement potential. The past record of stability may provide a valid indirect measure of survival potential, and we may have to resort to such data in order to operationalize this concept, but it is the probability of future pattern maintenance (survival of the system is an essential characteristic) that would determine most directly the ability of the system to progress toward its goals.

The responsive capacity of the system refers to its ability to respond effectively and efficiently to needs and problems arising in society or in the general environment of the political system. The response is in the form of policy outputs designed to meet these needs or solve these problems. What constitutes a need or a problem is defined by the goals or purposes of the political system, discussed in the previous section. The notion of responsiveness used here does not imply a simple stimulus-response relationship. It is conceived, rather, as a broad term covering all actions of governments in allocating values for society, including long-range plans, short-range policies, appropriations, and executive and judicial decisions. In focusing on the legislative system we are, of course, essentially interested in responses that are in the form of policies, appropriations, and other similar enactments.

The concept of institutionalization in this model needs some rather detailed explanation. My definition diverges from that employed in most of the literature on political development, as it is intended to avoid a "modernity" bias that is implicit in the notion of development. Essentially, I would define institutionalization as a rationalization of political structures to bring them into congruence with social structures and to maximize the communication flow between the political institutions and the social environment. This view follows Eisenstadt (1963) in recognizing that the increasing complexity and differentiation of a society lays the basis for political differentiation, but I do not regard the latter as synonymous with institutionalization. The two are related; we can expect that a highly institutionalized political system in a highly differentiated society would also have to be highly differentiated. But the two concepts are related in a rather complex way. Political differentiation might be considered a condition of institutionalization but one whose threshold value varied according to the degree of social differentiation. Or, if we were considering degrees of institutionalization, then the effect of the level of political differentiation would vary according to the level of social differentiation. This means that, at a constant level of political differentiation, its contribution to institutionalization would be inversely related to the degree to which it lagged social differentiation and directly related to the degree of congruence between them. Thus, a moderate element of institutionalization may be present even in more traditional societies where the level of social differentiation is low as long as the gap between it and political differentiation is not very great. We have therefore hypothesized a combined but opposing effect of the two differentiation variables on institutionsalization. In addition it might be expected that, at very low absolute levels of political differentiation, we would predict a low level of institutionalization regardless of whether the lag behind social differentiation was short or long. This assumption derives from a realization that it is not very meaningful to regard political structures as institutionalized in very primitive societies where there has been almost no development of any type, even though in a technical sense there might be zero lag between social and political differentiation.

In this discussion we are taking political differentiation to mean the functional differentiation of the parts of the political system. This also means not only that governmental functions, such as legislative, integrative, representative, and administrative, are clearly defined and differentiated and the role behavior related to the function clearly prescribed but also that there is further functional specification within each of these major functions. When we use the term "congruence" of political structure with social structure, it is essentially this latter form of differentiation with which we are concerned. At a minimum, institutionalization requires some degree of differentiation of major functions, but higher levels of institutionalization will require a matching of the structural complexity of government with that of society. Hence, the functional specialization that emerges in the social and economic systems would be reflected to some extent in the organization of units within the political system. This conceptualization is similar to that of Eckstein's notion of congruence, although his is essentially confined to similarities between the authority patterns of social and governmental units (1969: 290-300). I would give this a different emphasis, however, and focus on the structural congruence that permitted the optimum level of communication and interfacing between the social and governmental unit. Similarity of authority patterns may tend to enhance communication and interaction between the two, but that is not the crucial factor. The type of institutionalization that we are referring to is the institutionalization of the channels of communication and avenues of access, and the structural congruity is one that results from the mutual accommodations between governmental and social units to establish and maintain these patterns of interaction. This congruity can, in principle, be just as great in simpler societies with less elaborate political structures if the boundary exchanges between the social and political spheres are regularized and orderly, that is, if the roles and norms of the actors involved are well established and clearly defined. In this respect, therefore, we are concerned with what we might call institutionalization of behavior at the boundaries.

In another respect, our conception of institutionalization includes internal arrangements within and between structures of the political system. Here we move closer to the more conventional definitions of the term, but I choose to rely more on Harold Lasswell's formulations than on those more closely associated with the political development field. The latter carry with them too much of the Weberian and Parsonian baggage, which may have some relevance for analyzing bureaucracies but is less meaningful when fosucing on the legislative institution. The internal institutionalization we are here defining cannot be specified in any great detail, and to some extent its features will have to remain hypothetical. Clearly the governmental process requires more than a well-developed system of external and internal communications, although this is basic. The structure of an institutionalized system would be one that, in processing the flow of information into and through the system, would facilitate and maximize the possibilities of rational choice. It would be one in which policy alternatives were considered in terms of the extent to which they would optimize the goals of the system (see Lasswell, 1963: 21-22). This conceptualization has structural implications, inter alia, for the system of representation; the role of political parties; the organization of staff services, the system of coordination, and the planning agencies of the executive; and the committee system, leadership structure, and the informational services of the legislators. The elaboration of structures for policy evaluation would clearly be an important feature of an institutionalized system according to this conceptualization. What some of the more specific implications would be will be put off until we consider the operationalizing of this concept.

Integrative capacity relates to the ability of the system to confront the partial disintegration of society created by the process of social differentiation and to maintain consensus and support for the system by the many diverse groups in society. It is likely that some of the same structures responsible for the performance of the legislative function are involved in this function and that the effects of institutionalization on this will be similar to its effects on responsive capacity. We will not be particularly concerned with this concept here since it is not regarded as a capability of the legislative system as such, but, of course, it is important for the overall system and therefore needs to be included in the model.

Other concepts in the model are dealt with in the sections on interrelationships among and operationalizing of these concepts.

## INTERRELATIONSHIPS AMONG CONCEPTS

Let us now move forward through our model of the political system and discuss the hypothetical interrelationships among the system's concepts. It has already been noted that social differentiation lays the foundation for political differentiation. How does this process work? As a society becomes more "modernized," its structure generally becomes more complex, at least in respect to the proliferation of functional groupings within society. A vast variety and number of associations, interests, and institutions begin to emerge, mainly as a result of increasing industrialization with its concomitant increase in occupational specialization. The way in which these developments affect political institutions is undoubtedly quite complex, but one of the driving mechanisms behind the adaptations of the political system can be seen in the highly developed system of interest articulation and aggregation that eventuates from the highly differentiated societies. These systems abound with specialized interests that are cohesive and homogeneous, are relatively autonomous within their own functional areas, are typically well organized, and are run by institutionalized bureaucracies of their own. Most of these interests have succeeded in developing regularized and stable means of access to the political authorities. Another mechanism of adaptation springs from the compelling need for some degree of regulation and coordination of the diverse and far-flung spheres of power created by industrialization. This requires an increase in the scope of governmental power and, consequently, an increase in the complexity of government. Thus, the political system, in adapting to the changes in society, will tend to reflect the complexity of society as it seeks to accommodate the increasing intensity and variety of demands placed upon it.

In general the major development in the political system is an increasing functional specificity and autonomy of roles. This is particularly seen in the bureaucracies of developed countries, which tend to be highly specialized, in which relationships are precisely defined and delimited, and where a considerable degree of autonomy exists within their defined spheres of competence. But it might also be seen in the legislative system. In the more "developed" polities there would be presumably a clearer differentiation of the legislative function within the total system and a higher level of functional specialization within the legislative system. The legislative function would, thus, be more clearly recognizable and the boundaries of the legislative system, more sharply defined. Subunits within the legislative system—for example, committees, service agencies—would be highly specialized in terms of policy and skills and would maintain a certain degree of autonomy in the performance of their specialized roles. The result of this differentiation in the legislative system is, to the extent that it closely follows and "fits" the differentiation in society, to lay the basis for the institutionalization of the system.

In discussing differentiation, our assumption has been that the political always lags the social because the latter is presumed to be the initiating cause of the former. Such an assumption may seem to overlook the fact that a large number of relatively undifferentiated societies, particularly in Latin America and Africa, have instituted rather complex political systems patterned after those of the United States or European countries. But, in the actual operation of these systems, are they really very highly differentiated? I think most area specialists would agree that they are not. Many of the "legislatures" do not legislate; there is little bureaucratic specialization; judicial systems are not autonomous; and the scope of governmental power is restricted. Many of these systems are very unstable and readily revert to undifferentiated military dictatorships. One interpretation of their failure might be that the institution-building leadership was not sufficiently aware of this connection between social and political differentiation in its desire to "leap ahead" of social conditions by designing institutions that were, in a sense, too advanced for the development of society.[1]

We move ahead now to consider the complex of factors impinging directly on the dependent variable. To begin with, survival potential is hypothetically related to a number of factors which will be categorized under three headings. Barring foreign invasion, acts of God, and other catastrophes, these are the following: (1) features of the system which contribute to positive support for the system, (2) factors that tend to neutralize opposition to the system, and (3) time-related, legitimizing factors that solidify support and consensus for the regime. The first of these categories represents a specific application of the nothing-succeeds-like-success principle and is represented in part by the dotted feedback line in Figure 1 going from "goal achievement potential" to "survival potential." This connotes a feedback of specific support for the regime that directly contributes to its longevity when the system is actually moving forward with specific actions to reach its goals. Positive support is also represented by the line from "responsive capacity." This is more in the nature of diffuse support. When responsive capacity is high, there is a greater probability of consensus about the legitimacy of the system. Even without much progress toward goal achievement, if the system is perceived as being responsive to needs and attempting to solve problems, support would presumably be generated for the regime.

The second type of factor affecting survival potential tends to increase longevity by neutralizing opposition to the system. This is represented by the arrow going from "integrative capacity," which denotes the ability of structures within the system to incorporate, coopt, or otherwise integrate within the system potential opposition to the regime as such. This result is achieved through the system of representation, the institutionalization of channels of access and communication between the social and political systems, the provision of an official forum for opposition, the aggregative effects of political parties, and the process of political socialization. This integrative function is often the most significant non-legislative function performed by elected assemblies. The model indicates that integrative capacity affects goal achievement potential both indirectly, through survival potential, and directly. The direct path connotes the need for consensus to ensure the successful carrying out of public policy. Where integrative capacity is low, irreconcilable groups may well block or impede the effectiveness of solutions even after they have been adopted by the authorities. The level of integrative capacity is determined primarily by the degree to which the political system is institutionalized. In this regard, the characteristics of institutionalization that achieve a correspondence between the social and the political system and enhance the communications flow between the two systems are of considerable importance.

The third category of factors affecting survival potential—time-related, legitimizing influences—is represented in the model as the "age factor." In some sense this might be regarded as a residual category, but it is intended to be more than this. The basic conception was that there is something purely and directly related to the age of a system that contributes to the potential for survival; that structures and patterns of behavior, after some period of time, become valued, in part, merely because of their age; they become traditions rather than mere expectations. Perhaps a human generation would represent the threshold period of time in the operation of this process because of a probable tendency to accept with less questioning structures inherited from previous generations compared to those created in our own time. It takes a long time for the processes of political socialization to bear fruit. It also takes time to acquire a history, heroes, and a heritage. The institutions that belong to this history are to be cherished rather than questioned and to be defended because they are part of our past, part of our culture, and therefore a little part of us. Consequently the age factor is considered to be a separate variable in determining the survival potential of a system.

If survival potential is a function of the age of the system, it is undoubtedly a very complicated function. It is apparently nonlinear, and there may be a reversal of direction involved. As noted above, it might be assumed that age had no effect for the first approximately 25 years, or about a generation. Hence, the curve of regression would be flat for that length of tiem, but after this it would rise in a positive direction. At some point later on—100 years? 200 years?— it would flatten out again and might even descend in a negative direction as the process of ossification and decay begin to set in. How we might measure the age factor and determine the nature of this function will be discussed below when we deal with the means of operationalizing the model.

Let us consider now the other major variable affecting goal achievement, responsive capacity. This is essentially a measure of how well the overall system is responding to needs arising in the environment as determined by actual performance of the system and, in the scheme presented in Figure 1, is presumed to be affected mainly by institutionalization. It is also affected by unspecified social conditions, as are all the elements of the model, although these are not represented in the diagram. We will have to specify some of these conditions later on in testing the model, although they are not of central concern to us here. Institutionalization, however, is very central as it is conceived to be a major attribute of all structures within the political system. Our hypothesis is that the relationship between institutionalization and responsive capacity is direct, positive, and essentially linear. The greater the extent that political structures reflect and accommodate the differentiated structures of society, facilitate the flow of communications between society and the polity, are interrelated and internally constituted for a rational processing of inputs, the greater will be the responsive capacity of the system.

The three factors therefore that are hypothetical determinants of goal achievement potential are survival potential, integrative capacity, and responsive capacity. Of these, responsive capacity is assumed to be the most important; it is the key variable that fundamentally determines the overall performance of the system; and it is here that one would focus in making efforts to improve or "reform" the system.

A second feedback path is shown in Figure 1, this one going from "goal achievement potential" to "institutionalization." There may be other such feedback routes that one might suggest, but the two shown are regarded as the most obvious. This second path is indicative of feedback of information to the political structures on progress toward goals and provides the bases for further rationalization of these structures. This initiates a process that is similar to what Deutsch calls "resteering" of the system, although this is more of a "restructuring" of the system after information is fed back on how well the system is performing.

## OPERATIONALIZING CONCEPTS

In this section and in the next one, which is concerned with testing the model, we will focus more sharply onto the legislative system as a part of the political system. In respect to the model in Figure 1, this means we will concentrate mainly on the paths that lead to and from "responsive capacity," which is considered to be the key variable in the performance

of the legislative system. We will also concentrate on the institutionalization and differentiation of the legislative system structures rather than
other structures within the political system. Since the model was designed
in such a way that all concepts could be operationalized, all of these will
be touched upon in this section, but it is not feasible at this point to
attempt a testing of the entire model. In testing the legislative-system
aspect of the model, we will simply have to make a number of assumptions
about other aspects of the model, which hopefully will not be too far
from empirical reality.

### SOCIAL DIFFERENTIATION

First, let us give consideration to operationalizing the concept of
social differentiation. This might be defined operationally as a widespread
distribution of certain social characteristics among the population of the
political unit. Distributional statistics could therefore be used in measuring
this. Examples of this might be Gini coefficients of income distribution,
the distribution of the working population into occupational categories,
or the distribution of levels of educational attainment among the adult
population. Membership statistics in trade associations and labor unions
would also be useful. Economic measures that are correlated with social
differentiation could provide indirect indicators. These would include
measures of industrial diversification, per capita GNP, and per capita
consumption of fossil fuels. Since the concept of social differentiation
is fairly inclusive and may have a number of dimensions to it, it seems
advisable to use multiple indicators in measuring it. Lieberson (1969) has
put forward a convenient method of combining several measures of population diversity into a single index. Factor analysis, of course, might be
used if we had a rather large number of variables which logically seemed to
be related to different dimensions of this concept.

### POLITICAL DIFFERENTIATION

In order to operationalize political differentiation we must look to
measures of system complexity. We might use such gross measures as the
number of governmental units and subunits, or the number of governmental employees per 1,000 population; but if we focus more sharply on
the legislative system, we should be able to come up with some more
refined measures. We ought not only to have an indicator of how much
division and subdivision of structures existed but also a determination of
how clearly defined and stable it was. What is needed, in other words, is a
measure of the true level of functional specialization within the system.
To begin with, one would want to know how functionally specific

was the law-making or policy-making function, then to what extent this function was subdivided into various specialities. Thus, one would first determine if there was a body that specialized in law-making for the system and how authoritative and autonomous this body was. To what extent did its actions affect the behavior of others in the political and social systems? How much control did it have over its own internal processes and structures? It might be necessary to use some indirect measures here that would be indicative of the significance of the output and autonomy of this legislative body. For example, we could look at the amount of time spent in the deliberation on major legislation, the attendance during debate and during the votes on the legislation, the extent to which bills were revised and amended and budgets altered during the legislative process, or the total length and frequency of legislative sessions. With sufficient funds, of course, one could conduct interviews with legislators regarding the importance they attached to their legislative roles, or with their constituents to determine the level of prestige or respect they attributed to the legislative body. The amount of pay that the legislators received might also be a valid, indirect measure of how well they were regarded, as well as how much autonomy they possessed.

As a direct measure of formal autonomy, one might make an extensive list of all the matters that could possibly be subject to internal control and give each legislative body a score based on the proportion of the total that were actually internally controlled. Such a list might include session length and frequency, leadership qualifications and selection methods, the calendar, committee structure, voting rules and means of amending ills, the waiving of formal rules to expedite legislation, calling itself into session, censuring or expelling members, and determining legislative election district boundaries. Among the more indirect measures would be the amount of turnover attributable to defeat of incumbents at the polls. (Incumbents in the autonomous bodies should be better able to protect themselves against this kind of catastrophe.) Another indirect measure of internal control would be the amount of funds that the legislature spends on itself. These would be highest in the autonomous systems.

The second step in measuring the degree of differentiation of the law-making function would be to examine the number of functionally specific units involved in the performance of this function. Such units could be defined according to standards of authority and autonomy similar to those just discussed in relation to the legislative body as a whole. In regard to this kind of differentiation, we would want to direct our attention especially to committee systems, to party organizational structure within the legislative body, and to auxiliary service agencies connected with the legislature.

In devising some empirical measures of institutionalization, one has to be careful so as to avoid measuring political differentiation instead. It is important to keep these concepts quite distinct if one is to conform with the model. We will, of necessity, have to examine some of the same structural components in measuring institutionalization as political differentiation, but we will be looking at different attributes or aspects of these structures.

The concept of institutionalization presented here singles out two facets of political institutions. One involves the political system's relationships with its environment or other systems; and in this respect we are concerned with the openness of the political structures, the degrees of access to them, the channels of communication between them and the outside, and, in a sense, the extent to which they are integrated with the social system. The other facet involves the rationalization of internal relationships and processes in the system in a way that most effectively utilizes the information flowing into the system and weights the various interests making demands on the system. In discussing how to operationalize these two facets, we will first consider what will be regarded as the "normal" situation, which is one in which the legislature plays a major role in the law-making function. Then we will consider how these facets might be measured where this function is preempted by other institutions.

As one measure of the first facet, we would look again toward the committee system in legislatures where committees play a significant role, and here we would seek to devise some indicators of the openness of this system. The volume of transactions between the public, including interest group representatives, and the committees could be measured. The total amount of time consumed in taking public testimony or the proportion of time spent in open, public session compared with that spent in executive sessions might be used as an indicator. The structure of the relationship between the individual member of the legislative body and his constituency should also be examined in terms of his accessibility and the information flow between them. Time allocation studies could be made of the amount of attention the legislators give to information on the needs of their constituencies related to legislation, and the volume of transactions could be measured. The extent of the informational staff services provided to legislators and legislative committees would also provide a partial index of this concept. The number of officially recognized legislative lobbyists in the capital might also be used, or any measure of the total amount of participation in the legislative system by those who were not members of the legislative bodies themselves.

Another aspect of the openness of the system relates to the openness of the recruiting for legislative roles. This view may seem contrary to the usual conceptualization of institutionalization. According to Polsby, for example, "As an organization institutionalizes, it stabilizes its membership, entry is more difficult, and turnover is less frequent" (1968: 146). This seems to connote a rather "closed" system. Admittedly, there is some conceptual tension between the notion of open recruiting and the requirement that an institutionalized structure be manned by specialists and persons capable of rationally analyzing the problems of public policy. Still, there is no need for conflict here; the openness in the recruiting process refers to the absence of artificial, unreasonable, or dysfunctional barriers to entry. What would be maximized, accoridng to my conception of institutionalization, is the closeness of the relationship between society and the political system, and a recruiting system that would accomplish this would be unbiased as to the entry of various classes, occupational groupings, ethnic, racial, and religioius groups, and the like. The need to know the needs of various segments of society is very important in this conceptualization, for, as A. D. Lindsay (1947: 269) has put it, "Only the wearer knows where the shoe pinches." Thus, even a relatively "untutored" individual could be an expert or a specialist in the problems of the group to which he belongs.

A reasonably valid indirect measure of the openness of the recruiting process might be the extent to which the distribution of socioeconomic characteristics of the membership of legislative bodies matched that of society in general. Of course, the match will never be very close; the "upper" or better educated classes will almost always be overrepresented, but there should be some substantial relative differences between political systems. Membership turnover statistics might be used, but the consequences of and the factors behind variance in turnover are quite ambiguous. A high rate of turnover would seem to preclude development of some types of functional specialization within the system, although it would also bring into the system "fresh" viewpoints and possibly more intimate knowledge of social problems. More useful would be careful studies of legislative recruitment patterns such as that by Kornberg, Clarke, and Watson (1973) on the Canadian Parliament.

Finally, the openness of the legislative system is dependent to a great extent on the manner in which political parties are organized both outside and inside the legislative bodies. The openness of the party recruitment process could be measured as Eldersveld (1964) did in Michigan, but for comparative analysis it is probably more manageable to examine the extensiveness or the degree of geographical disperison of the party organization throughout the country. We would want to know how far and to what extent the tentacles of the party reached into the grass roots of the social system. The open party would tend to have the characteristics of the "mass" party, as described by Duverger (1951: 63-71) rather than the "cadre" party. It would have some sort of organization down to the smallest political unit in the system and would welcome one and all to its ranks. In the legislature, those allied with such a party would, presumably, be in closer touch with public needs and problems than the members of the more remote and aloof cadre parties. The organization of parties within the legislative bodies would be considered open if there was widespread participation in party affairs and policies of the party. The more decisions that were made by party caucus, the more open the party would be. The less autocracy and centralization, the more open the party. The members of such a party would, therefore, tend to be more equal in their influence over party matters and decisions than the members of closed parties. This notion does not conflict with conditions for functional specialization; members of open parties could be superior in their influence within their own areas of expertise, but the power exerted by the general leadership of the party would not be extensive. It seems to me, however, that it does conflict with the notion that the use of the "seniority rule" in the selection of leadership is evidence of institutionalization (Polsby, 1968: 160-64). This is confusing institutionalization with ossification. Such a rule can be a deterrent to openness and institutionalization, as I conceive it. In an open system, leadership roles would be determined more by knowledge and achievement, and selection would be as democratic as feasible.

The strength or cohesion of the party organizations within the legislative bodies is related to institutionalization but in a rather complex manner. It is regarded here as a nonlinear, interactive relationship, which is explicated by the following propositions:

(1) The level of institutionalization of the legislative system varies positively with variations in party cohesion or control to the extent that party structure is more open and rationalized than nonparty legislative structures; where the latter are more open and rationalized, variations in party cohesion or control will be negatively related to institutionalization.

(2) The level of institutionalization of the legislative system varies positively with variations in the openness and rationality of nonparty legislative structures to the extent that party cohesion or control of the formal legislative bodies is weak or nonexistent; where such

cohesion or control is strong, the degree to which variations in openness and rationality of legislative structures
produce variations in institutionalization is accordingly
reduced.

The logic behind these propositions is that under conditions of strong party
control the law-making function is removed, in a sense, from the formally
constituted arena of decision-making; therefore, the structural characteristics of that arena are not of very great importance in the legislative process,
but the characteristics of the party structure become highly significant.
Further on, when the testing of the model is described, the significance
of these relationships should become apparent.

Next let us consider the measurement of the internal institutionalization of the legislative system, or the degree of rationalization of the system.
We will deal with two aspects of this: (1) the system of representation,
and (2) the decision-making processes. An equitable method of representation in the legislative system is clearly consistent with our concept of
rationalization and institutionalization since it would help to assure that
the needs of all segments of society were known, that no major interests
or problem areas were ignored, and that the resolution of problems did
not unduly damage the interests of any segment. No system of representation could guarantee such results, of course, but a reasonably equitable
system would seem to be a necessary condition in order to achieve these
aims. What would seem to be important here, regardless of the method of
election, is that each member of the public have roughly equal influence
in the selection of representatives. The concept of "one man, one vote"
embodies this fairly well, and deviations from this ideal can be measured
quite feasibly (see Schubert and Press: 1964).

As regards the legislative processes that lead to the most rational
decisions, we are in a realm of some uncertainty and speculation and can
only put forward some rather tentative notions of what rationalization
means in this respect. The ancient problem of majority will versus minority rights might be raised here, as well as the question of the existence of
a "general will" and how it is to be discovered. Even if we accept the
proposition that there are general, universal goals that are known for the
political system, there is still a great deal of latitude for public policy
directed toward these goals and, conceivably, a wide variety of institutional arrangements that could produce such policies. Nevertheless, if
we are further willing to accept the rationality criterion for institutionalized structures, then we may be able to define these structures somewhat
more specifically. Rationality, in this context, requires (1) complete
information about the problem or condition of need in society, a complete

description of the problem, its causes, and its effects on individual segments of society; (2) a full exploration of all alternative solutions to the problem and prediction of the probable total consequences or "utilities" of each alternative; and (3) selection of the solution that optimizes the set of values adopted by the system. This is an ideal notion of rationality and, obviously, one that would never exist in reality; and so we should be willing to accept something like Simon's (1957) conception of "bounded rationality," which substitutes "satisfying" for "optimizing." This predicts that a decision will be adopted when an alternative seems to meet minimal standards, or is "good enough," and that we cannot depend on the availability of all possible alternatives from which the best may be selected. But whether we are looking for the best solution or merely a satisfactory solution, we will still want to get as much information as practical on the nature of the problem, possible alternatives, and probable consequences.

What are the implications of this notion of rationality for legislative structures? It means that there would be structural arrangements that would seek to maximize the flow of information into the system and provide for the most thorough and objective processing and analyzing of this information. The "open" system described in the previous section can provide the basis for the flow of information about the nature of the problem and possibly about some alternative solutions, but more than this is necessary. Committees and other subunits of the legislative system should be structured so that they can effectively process and analyze this information and gather further data and conduct inquiries on various solutions and their consequences. This means that committees would have adequate professional staffs, there would be well-equipped research and data-gathering agencies attached to the legislative bodies, and that individual members would have sufficient staff assistance to help them collect, analyze, and summarize the information they required to make a rational or satisfactory decision on legislation. Possibly a good summary of the extent to which this sort of service is provided is the amount of money the legislatures appropriate for informational, service, and research agencies and to staff committees and individual members, though this might have to be backed up with some indicator of the use of such agencies and staffs.

The structural prerequisites to satisfy the third requirement of rationality—that the opitmal solution is actually chosen—are even more difficult to define, except in a negative sense. Under this conception there would be no arbitrary barriers to adoption of the optimal solution. Some of the "checks and balances" of the U.S. legislative systems enhance the rationality of the system by providing delays for further analysis and study, a multistage examination of most legislative proposals, and the airing of many different interests and opinions. But they can also reduce the system's rationality by permitting single individuals or "veto" groups to block legislation that meets the test of rationality. Structures designed to expedite legislation may also tend to impede it or block it entirely—for example, the House Rules Committee. In a sense, these devices are being "misused" when legislation is killed by the will of one individual or small group who are in key positions of power within the system. So we cannot rely on the existence of various checks in the system as either a measure of rationality or nonrationality but would have to examine the actual incidence of their misuse. Eventually, however, we might also be able to discover which devices were most subject to abuse, and this then would permit us to use their existence in an index of nonrationality. This is about as far aw we can take this notion now, although we have not specifically discussed how to identify instances of "misuse." In a very tentative fashion, however, we might suggest some devices that might generally tend to further rationality rather than the opposite and then some that would generally tend to reduce rationality. In the first category might be put bicameralism (to the extent that it provides more thorough analysis of legislation), review of legislation by expert standing committees, multiple readings of bills, conference committees, and provision for discharge petitions. In the latter category we might put provision for unlimited debate, control over committee assignments by presiding officers, the seniority rule, executive veto of legislation, and constitutional limitations on length and frequency of legislative sessions.

Where there is some institutional separation of legislative and executive functions, there is one final matter to consider in measurement of institutionalization of legislative bodies, and that is the relationships between those institutions primarily involved in the executive function and those primarily involved in the legislative function. In an open, rational system, inputs from executive structures would be frequent and free flowing. Channels of communication would be well developed, and there would be a high volume of informational exchange between the two systems. Ordinarily we might not agree that an institutionalized legislative system was one that was dominated by the executive, although we must be careful about what we really would mean by this. To the extent that actors and institutions involved primarily in the executive function influence the policy decisions of legislative bodies, they become part of the legislative system. Our attention then would be shifted somewhat from the legislative bodies to executive structures. We would therefore have a situation analogous to that in which political parties or their leaders come to exert some control over legislative decisions. The institutionalization of the legislative system would begin to depend to some extent on the openness and rationality of executive institutions, and we would then want to examine these more closely for the presence of some of the same structural features we have been describing as requisite to the institutionalization of legislative bodies. We shall deal with these shortly.

As a variable, the strength of executive control over law making can be assumed to have the same kind of interactive effect on institutionalization as the strength of party control. In the propositions presented on page 30, one might simply substitute "executive control" for "party cohesion or control." Thus, variations in the strength of executive control result in a positive effect on institutionalization where executive institutions are open and rationalized and the formal legislative institutions are not, and a negative effect where the reverse is true. Furthermore, changes in formal legislative structures will affect institutionalization when executive control is weak but will have negligible effect when it is strong. These propositions are of considerable importance when we come to analyze the way in which institutional change affects responsive capacity and other variables in the system.

It may therefore be noted at this point that there are really two separate stages in the measurement of the institutionalization of the legislative function. The first of these is measurement of the degree to which a body known as the "legislature" is involved in the performance of the legislative function as compared to another institution, that is, most generally, the "executive." In the second stage one seeks to measure the openness and rationality of the institution or those institutions that play the dominant role in this function. It should normally not be very difficult to determine the degree of the legislature's autonomy with respect to the executive or, conversely, the extent of the executive's dominance of the legislative function. One has to be able to trace the initiation of legislative measures, which may pose some investigative problems, but once this is accomplished, indices of executive dominance may easily be constructed based on the volume and significance of legislative measures originating in the executive establishment and the treatment of such measures by the legislative body. In respect to the latter, we would want to know to what extent the measures were altered, amended, or rejected entirely, and the level of support and opposition the measures initiated by the executive received. The continuum established by this process would find those political systems based on separation of powers at one end representing "legislative-body autonomy," while parliamentary systems generally ruled by coalition cabinets might tend to be more toward the middle, and parliamentary systems with one party in the majority would be close to the other end representing "executive dominance." At still a further extreme from the latter would be systems in which there was no semblance of a legislative body or where such a body automatically ratified all executive decrees.

In this section on institutionalization we have considered in some detail the measurement of this concept only under the conditions where a body identified as having the normal characteristics of a "legislature" plays the dominant role in legislation. Where the executive is dominant in this respect, we have a somewhat more difficult task of measuring the openness and rationality of the relevant structures. Most viable legislatures conduct their business under rather close public scrutiny and keep comprehensive public records of their proceedings. Since their members are customarily elected, the processes by which they attain membership in this institution can be investigated with some facility. Also, the process by which leaders are selected can quite readily be examined. Background data about the legislators themselves is often abundantly available. The bureaucracy is not as accessible to examination. While it is true that some of the legislature's business is conducted in secret, there are very few processes in most executive institutions that are regularly available for public inspection.

Nevertheless, the many studies of bureaucracies (for a pertinent compendium, see Katz and Danet, 1973) show that they can yield to probing analysis. It should be possible to measure the degree of openness in executive agencies in a manner somewhat similar to that in legislative bodies. One should be able, for example, to analyze the transactions between executive officials and members of the public or pressure group representatives and examine the extent and nature of structures for the institutionalization of these contacts. In a number of U.S. federal agencies the structures for maintaining communication with "clientele" groups have been highly developed. Second, it should be feasible to study the recruitment of individuals to policy-making roles in the executive establishment. The most open systems would be those that showed a minimum of social class, ethnic, or racial bias in the recruitment to these roles. Such a condition of minimum bias is enhanced where achievement, rather than ascriptive norms, is the basis of selection, but it is not guaranteed. The presence of something similar to the "affirmative action programs" imposed upon U.S. institutions of higher education might further enhance this condition. Third, we can observe the degree of turnover of circulation among the higher level policy-making positions in the executive establishment. This would not be related to institutionalization in a linear fashion; rather, one would expect an optimum amount of turnover would be at a fairly moderate level. This optimum would be one that would enhance openness by virtue of bringing in "fresh" viewpoints from outside the bureaucracy but would not be such as to diminish the rationality of the system by unduly destroying the continuity of policy leadership. Deviations from that optimum in either

direction would thereby provide a measure of the lack of institutionalization of the system.

In the measurement of rationality, we are dealing with a more familiar
attribute of an "institutionalized" bureaucracy in the more traditional
sense of that term. Admittedly, the definition of institutionalization set
forth here, in that it emphasized openness as one criterion, is not consistent with this traditional sense—in fact, it may be in direct conflict with it.
But, since rationality is consistent wth this traditional sense, tools for
measuring it can be found among the vast literature of research on bureaucracies. It is too tangential to the purpose of this essay to delve into this
here, but we can mention some of the major lines of approach. It would be
necessary to examine the formal and, especially, informal organizational
structure within the executive institution, with particular concentration
on hierarchical patterns; the flow of communication upward, downward,
and horizontally; the job classification system; the recruitment and promotion system; structures for policy coordination; and the extent, nature,
and utilization of policy research, staff, and planning agencies. Since the
goal of increased rationality in executive decision making has guided much
of the research in the field of public administration in recent years, there
should now be a sufficient body of knowledge to inform us as to what the
structural characteristics are that contribute to this goal.

Another possibility of dominance by a structure other than the
legislature is that by a political party. Techniques for measuring the openness of party organizations have been developed, notably by Eldersveld
(1964). The main concern in this respect is the degree to which membership and leadership within the organization is open to the broadest cross
section of the population. In other words, the emphasis is on the openness
of the system of recruiting people as workers and to other positions
within the organization. One might also look toward the system of party
finance to determine how widely distributed was the financial support for
the party. Parties that received many individual contributions from a
broadly based portion of society might be considered more open than one
with few contributions, and these only from a narrow social segment.

Political parties have never been celebrated for the rationality of
their decision-making processes. They do not customarily have large staffs
for policy research, although these do exist in the British parties and some
of the continental socialist parties. The existence of such staffs would,
however, provide a possible indicator of rational policy making. Since
major public policy positions are often formulated by ad hoc committees
and ratified by conventions or other large representative groups, examination of the structure, composition, and processes of these committees
should provide the basis for constructing indicators of rationality in party

policy making. To some extent these bodies may be approached analytically in the same manner as legislative bodies.

## RESPONSIVE CAPACITY

Operationalizing the concept of responsive capacity constitutes a major effort of this paper. The lack of such a performance measure in past studies designed to evaluate legislative institutions has, I believe, seriously dimished their scientific and practical value. An extensive study of 50 state legislatures, for example, by the Citizens Conference on State Legislatures purported to "evaluate their effectiveness," but it examined structural characteristics of these legislatures and had no independent, objective criterion for "effectiveness." There is often the tendency to regard certain structural characteristics or procedures as "good" on simply an a priori basis (e.g., joint committees, a "consent" calendar, prior introduction of bills) and to speak of "reforms" of the legislative system while possessing very little knowledge of the real consequences of these "reforms" for the performance of the system. Much of the literature on political development also suffers from unexamined premises about institutionalization and modernization. It is easy to assume that a so-called developed or institutionalized system will have a higher level of capacity than those that are not, but this should be a matter of empirical investigation. It would seem to be of utmost importance that we determine which features or types of institutionalization contribute to capacity and which do not.

Responsive capacity is defined here as the capabilities of the system, as measured by actual performance, to respond by appropriate public action to needs and problems created by manifest inequities and insecurities within society. More specifically, the responsive capacity of the legislative system can be measured by its performance in adopting policy, plans, and general programs that meet such needs. The measurement of responsive capacity, therefore, presents three problems that must be resolved: (1) how to measure variations in need or severity of the problem, (2) how to determine what response is appropriate, and (3) how to measure variations in effectiveness and efficiency of the response.

We will be guided in defining needs and problems by our explication of the goals of the state. A measurement of need would be the distance that the system is at a given point in time from fully achieving its goals. (It may never be possible to achieve the goals, but this can still serve as a reference point for measurement.) The "appropriate" response will be determined empirically. Lacking omniscience regarding how to solve all the problems of society, one has to resort to an examination of what is actually being done to solve the problems. What has been the general response to the needs of the system? Once we have determined the kind of response that is made to a given need, we can tell whether an individual system has responded or not and in most instances we will be able to scale the response in terms of some quantitative criterion. Then it should be possible to match the level of the response to the level of need and thereby construct an index of the effectiveness of the response.

Let us consider some examples to illustrate how one might proceed in the construction of such an index. First, the problem of financial inequalities is quite amenable to this kind of approach. The extremes of poverty and wealth in every country, even in the most developed, precipitate some kind of governmental action, however meager in some places, to redress these inequalities. Income distribution schemes have been adopted in most countries with capitalistic or mixed economies. Typically, these have taken the form of welfare programs involving direct payment by the state to individuals considered to be below a subsistence level of income. To measure need in this area, a Gini coefficient of income maldistribution is generally the most appropriate since it is a measure of the distance between what exists at a given time and an ideal condition or goal. A quantitative measure of the policy response might be the proportion of the population below the subsistence-income level who were receiving welfare payments, or the average amount of welfare payments, or a combination of these. Adjustments would have to be made for cross-national differences in living standards, but this can easily be accomplished.

Another example can be seen in the realm of educational policy. The distribution of educational attainment is easily measured, and an index of educational inequality can readily be constructed. The governmental response might be the programs seeking to equalize per-pupil expenditures across educational systems. Although Coleman (1966) and some recent studies in Sweden have raised questions about the consequences of this approach, this is the typical response, and it probably represents the only feasible approach a central government can take where there is any degree of decentralization of the educational system. The per capita amounts expended by the central government for the purposes of achieving equalization could be used as the measure of the level of response.

A final example would be in the area of health care. Extraordinarily high morbidity and mortality rates in a community or wide variations in the rates from one segment of society to another suggest the need for the political system to respond. The response would be the initiation of, or increased support for, public health and hospital programs, or a more comprehensive system of publicly financed medical care. Once again, measurement of need is straightforward and can be based on morbidity and mortality statistics. The magnitude of the response might be measured by the per capita amounts appropriated for various health programs.

Table 1 represents ten hypothetical sets of need-response variables for various policy areas. This is only a suggested list and possibly more could be added to it. It is important that all areas of public policy should be included as far as possible. These are designated as hypothetical sets of variables because, before they are incorporated into an overall responsive capacity index, we need some empirical evidence that the policy variable is the appropriate response to the need variable. A logical way to obtain this evidence would be to take a sample of states or all of the states in a particular study and examine whether the policy response is indeed the typical or normal response to the condition of need. More specifically, this might be done by correlating changes in need with the hypothesized change in policy. Most of these variables could be measured on an interval scale, and one could establish a level for rejecting the hypothesis that the response was the appropriate one.

Correlating needs and responses performs another very important function in our scheme. We can use the residuals from the regression line of such an analysis as the first approximation of a responsiveness index. The rationale behind this is as follows: the existence of a need is considered to be the initiating cause of a response intended to remedy the need. Variations in level of need across systems would presumably account variations in the response of these systems, but would not account for all such variations. There would consequently be an "unexplained variance" in the responses as a result of the effect of factors other than need. Our operating assumption is that, on the whole, these factors constitute the determinants of the system's responsiveness. Another way of viewing this is to say that we are analyzing responses while holding needs constant—that is, as if needs were equal for all systems.

Clearly, we have a rather gross index of responsiveness here, one that would include system factors as well as factors outside the system. We really need to exclude the latter if we want a purer measure of system responsiveness. Furthermore, we may be faced here with a problem of reciprocal causation; we can never be sure, when using simple cross-sectional analysis, how much of the covariance between need and response is a function of the feedback effect of the policy on the conditions of need. This problem is a particularly critical one in this sort of analysis because the policies adopted in response to needs would presumably be ones designed to reduce the level of need. Thus, the covariance produced by this feedback effect would be of the opposite sign from that produced by the effects of need on response and thereby would tend to depress the correlation of response against need. In order to partial out this reciprocal effect, it is necessary to add a longitudinal or dynamic dimension to the analysis by time-lagging the data and by utilizing percentage-change statistics instead of a measure of static conditions. We would therefore measure the percentage increase or decrease in an environmental variable—

**Table 1. Needs and responses in the legislative system**

### Goal of Equality

| Environmental Needs | Policy Response |
|---|---|
| 1. Gini index of income distribution. | 1. Tax progressiveness indices:<br>(a) based on average slope of Lorenz curve of percentage of income derived from various income categories in the income tax:<br>(b) degree of reliance on most progressive tax. |
| 2. Index of inequality of local school district expenditures. | 2. Central government (state) aid to local school districts. |
| 3. Housing segregation score. | 3. Liberality of fair-housing legislation. |

### Goal of Security and Order

| Environmental Needs | Policy Response |
|---|---|
| 1. Crime rates. | 1. Expenditures for police protection, crime prevention, corrections, and rehabilitation. |
| 2. Percentage of population with incomes less than subsistence level. | 2. Welfare-liberalism index: derived by factor analysis from quantitative variables related to welfare policy, such as percentage of welfare recipients in population, average monthly payment per recipient, and per capita expenditures on welfare. Index corrected for differences in standard of living. |
| 3. Index of public health: composite of infant mortality rate, life expectancy at age 60, number of physicians per 10,000 population, number of hospital beds per 10,000 population, general mortality rate, and percentage of draftees failing medical examination. | 3. Public expenditures for health and hospitals and medical care. |
| 4. Index of social malaise: composite of suicide rate, drug addiction rate, alcoholism rate, draftees failing mental requirements, crimes against persons, rate of unemployment, percentage of work time lost through strikes, and illegitimacy index. | 4. Public expenditures for mental health, expenditures for parks and recreation, and liberality index of civil rights legislation. |
| 5. Gross national (state) product per capita. | 5. Expenditures on public works, roads, and business subsidies per capita. |
| 6. Total annual investment in new plant and equipment per capita. | 6. Direct public investment in business and industry and indirect public investment through tax system per capita. |

the proportion of the population with incomes less than subsistence level, for example—over a period of years. Then we would measure the change in the relevant policy variable over approximatley the same length of time, but the period would have its beginning point a few years later. How much later and the length of the time period for measuring change in the variables are subjects we will investigate below.

The other problem with our index of responsiveness, that nonsystem factors may account for some of the residual variance when response is regressed against need, can be solved in a more conventional manner. Let us assume, for example, that economic conditions within the polity affect to some extent the capacity of the political system to respond to needs. In such circumstances a particular political system itself might be highly responsive, but it may not have the economic resources to make an adequate response to the need: therefore, if we find that the first residuals are correlated with economic development, we would want to control additionally for this economic variable. Other environmental factors may also be correlated with the residuals, and these should also be controlled. Separate analyses of each of the need-response areas would have to be made to determine what exogenous variables needed to be partialed out, and it should be recognized that nonsystem factors for one policy area might be considered system factors in another. Economic development, for example, would be a system variable with respect to the goal of economic security. We would seek, therefore, to produce in each policy area a responsiveness index whose variance was accounted for only by system factors.

Indices would be constructed for each of the individual policy areas, but these all could be combined into an overall responsiveness score for the system. One might not have very great confidence in the reliability of individual policy area scores, but one could generally expect the overall index to be highly reliable.

Because responsive capacity is such a central concept in the model proposed here, it may be well to discuss ways in which this capacity might be measured and to indicate why this particular approach was deemed most valid. Viewed in terms of the Eastonian systems framework, we have reached about as far back into the political process as one possibly could in using environmental indicators as initiating factors in the process. A more direct approach might be to match up demands with response, since what appear to be needs might never produce any demands for an authoritative reallocation of values. But it is too narrow a definition of the legislative function to regard it as one that involves only a response on a rather direct one-to-one basis to demands placed upon it. This sort of simplistic stimulus-response model has long been considered obsolete in behavioral psychology and also appears to be conceptually inadequate for a legislative systems analysis. The conceptualization of responsiveness that I have put forth includes the notion of innovation. As an ideal type, a responsive and innovative legislative system is one that anticipates problems or future demands; it seeks to correct inequities even when the pressures to do so have not yet reached a crisis level; it does not rely entirely on interests outside the legislative system to pressure it into action but seeks through its own sources information about conditions of need in society. A measuring instrument, therefore, that starts with needs and ends up with a policy output will encompass what we would consider to be the entire legislative process and provide an index of responsive capacity for that total process.

One other approach is to take public opinion on a given issue as an indicator of need for a policy responses and then match this with the actual response. Weber and Shaffer (1970) have adopted this approach in a study of the relationships between simulated public opinion data and policy response in a number of issue areas for the 50 American states. Although this might be regarded as a general measure of responsiveness, it is more a measure of "democraticness" or, at best, of a democratic type of responsiveness. What one is measuring here is the degree to which the legislative system responds to the so-called will of the people. This certainly is one way of evaluating legislatures, but it is not as universal a criterion as one involving an objective measurement of need. If we are attempting to apply our evaluative criteria to the vast variety of political systems, western and nonwestern, traditional and transitional, developing and developed, totalitarian and liberal-democratic, by adopting their approach we have already prejudged most of the systems and are left with the possibility of only delineating the differences between a small number of "democratic" systems. Furthermore, this approach, since it confounds democraticness with responsiveness, forecloses on the possibility of asking the question: Are the more democratic legislative systems more responsive than the less democratic? That is a question that, in principle, could be answered where responsiveness depends on an objective indicator of need.

### GOAL ACHIEVEMENT POTENTIAL

In one sense, goal achievement potential carries the notion of response capacity one step further. Whereas the latter spans the political process from the existence of an environmental need to a response designed to meet that need, the former concept incorporates the final or "impact" stage of the process and calls for analysis of the consequences or effects of the policy response. In order to operationalize this concept, it is necessary to determine not only whether there was a response designed to meet a need but whether that response actually brought about an improvement in the conditions defining the need. One might say that with responsive capacity we were concerned with *outputs* and here we are concerned with *outcomes*. One wants to know in this context: Do the outpus of the system actually move us forward toward the goals of the system? A system may be highly responsive in that it assiduously confronts the needs and problems of society and puts forth a steady and concerted effort to ameliorate these needs or to solve these problems, but there may be a breakdown in the system between its output and the intended impact of the output. The good intentions of the policy makers may have paved the road to a disaster or to something quite unexpected. This breakdown might be the result of a badly designed policy, poor implementation, an intractable environment, or some random or catastrophic event that destroys the operations of the policy.

The actual measurement of goal achievement potential can be accomplished in a fashion similar to that used in the measurement of responsive capacity. We start by measuring the level of need at time-$t_0$ and the same at time-$t_1$. The difference represents the amount of progress made toward goal achievement, and the difference divided by the elapsed time, the rate of progress. In the "rate of progress' we have a rough measure for comparing systems in regard to their capabilities to achieve their goals, but the measure can be refined. To begin with, there should be an adjustment for a predictable slowing down of the rate of progress as systems come closer to their goals. Presumably this decline in rate would result from a lessening of pressures for remedial action as the magnitude of need diminished, and a tendency in some policy areas for a given amount of effort to produce an ever smaller effect as the ideal state is approached. The adjustment can perhaps best be made empirically and by turning again to regression analysis. We would regress level of need at $t_1$ against the level at $t_0$ and use the residuals from the resulting regression line as the adjusted measure of the rate of progress. We should not assume linearity in this analysis; in fact, one would predict a leveling off of the regression line as the magnitude of need became relatively small. A curvilinear function should therefore be fitted to the data, and the residuals should be taken from this. The height of a point on the regression curve represents the level that would be achived at the end of the time period by the average system for the respective initial level of need. At any given initial level of need, systems falling below the regression line would be making faster than average progress toward goal achievement, and thos above, slower progress. A hypothetical form of this curve is depicted in Figure 2.

As with responsive capacity, we would like to purify our measuring

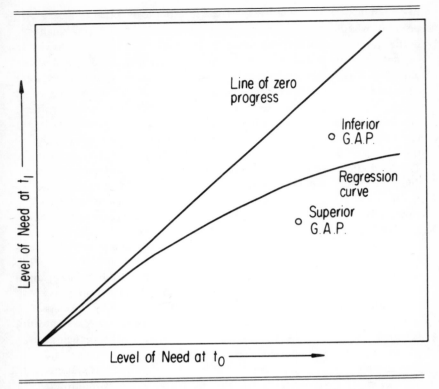

Figure 2. *Hypothetical regression curve for computing goal achievement potential*

device of nonsystem factors. Again, one has to consider that each policy area is, in a sense, a separate system and recognize that what is a non-system factor in one area is a system factor in another. Thus a state may be impeded from making satisfactory progress toward educational equality in part because of the underdeveloped nature of its economy, which would be a nonsystem factor in this policy area, but with respect to the goal of achieving economic security, the condition of the economy becomes an important endogenous variable. In the final analysis, the composite index should reflect goal achievement potential in all of the areas over which the state has some control. If variables affected by state action are factored out in constructing some components of the index, they would reappear in the construction of an appropriate component.

   There are some additional nonsystem factors that intervene between the policy response of the system and its impact on the environment if we are concerned only with an evaluation of the legislative system. In particular the effectiveness of the administration and application of a policy would be such nonsystem factors, that is, not a part of the legislative function. If such effectiveness could be quantified, it ought to be partialed out of an index designed to measure goal achievement potential of the legislative system only. Other nonsystem factors mentioned below would also be partialed out, as would survival potential and integrative capacity. This, obviously, becomes overly complex, and with so many variables controlled it is likely to become a rather unreliable measure. Furthermore, as the additional variables were controlled, the index would come more and more to look like responsive capacity. Theoretically, the only difference that could result between them would be from use of a policy response in constructing the latter that was inappropriate or by its nature ineffective in meeting the particular need involved. These considerations lead to the suggestion that, in testing the model with a view toward evaluation of legislative systems, responsive capacity is a satisfactory substitute for the ultimate dependent variable. If one uses responsive capacity, however, he must be concerned about selecting policy responses whose environmental impacts are as predictable as possible.

Goal achievement potential is conceived essentially, however, as a performance measure for the system as a whole. In view of this, one would not want to control for variables related to the application and administration of policy because these are involved in the output of the total system. Besides those that have already been mentioned, the only other nonsystem factors we would want to adjust for would be random events such as natural disasters. An earthquake might so damage the economy of a region that it caused a severe setback to the system in achieving some of its goals, despite the efforts (responses) that it might put forth. Such random events are difficult to handle systematically. All that can be said is that the investigator should be aware of the history of each state between $t_0$ and $t_1$. Where such disruptive events occur during this period, he should attempt to project whatever trends he discerns in the data in order to estimate what conditions would have been at $t_1$ had the event not occurred. This estimate would be used then in place of the actual value for the variable.

There are three more concepts in the model—integrative capacity, survival potential, and the age factor—which we will also pass over briefly because they are not involved in the legislative function directly. I shall suggest, however, how each of these might be operationalized. Integrative capacity can probably best be measured by its results, which are support for the regime and a maintenance of consensus regarding the values of the political system. These, in turn, could be measured either by survey methods (see Patterson, Wahlke, and Boynton, 1973) or by indices of domestic unrest and discontent (see Gurr, 1968). Since more of this capacity is needed in social environments that are highly differentiated in order to maintain a constant level of support or consensus, one should control for social differentiation in the construction of an integrative capacity index.

In order to measure survival potential, something akin to an actuarial study is necessary; and if we wish to test the full model, including this concept, this would mean that our universe of states would be those that are no longer in existence. Once the model has been verified, however, and the functional relationship between survival potential and the age factor has been determined, estimates of the value of this variable based on the age of the regime may be substituted in a formula for predicting goal achievement potential of existing systems.

An actuarial study of political systems could be made in the same way that life expectancy tables are constructed for human beings. One might proceed as follows: On the assumption that the universe of observations included only the modern nation-states, trace back to the beginning of the modern nation-state system and partition the period from then until the present into, say, ten-year or twenty-year periods. Within each one of these periods, count the political systems that survived and those that were radically altered, overthrown, or met their demise. Note the ages of the surviving systems at the midpoint of the period and the ages of the nonsurviving systems at the point of termination. One the basis of these data, calcualte the probability of demise at each year of age, or alternatively, the remaining life expectancy for each year of age. We would expect to find that the infant mortality rate for states would be rather high; but, in contrast to human beings, if middle age were achieved, remaining life expectancy would be increased. Eventually, however, the process of decay might set in, and the system would die of "old age." A curve based on such speculation about age of states and the life expectancy is shown in Figure 3.

One question that arises in this kind of analysis is: How do we know when a system has met its demise and a new system has come into being? The answer is to look for sudden or radical alterations in its structures. Evolutionary change, even though it was substantial, would not count. We would be looking for revolutionary change that abruptly overturned existing structures and replaced them with something quite different. This abrupt change in regime need not be accompanied by social revolution as was the Russian Revolution of 1917. The American Revolution would also qualify. The essential criterion signifying that change in regime has actually taken place is when none or very few of the valued symbols attached to

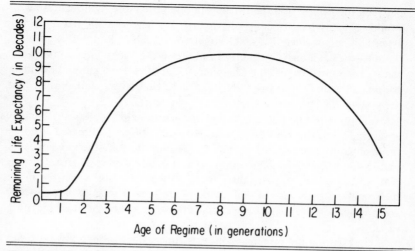

*Figure 3. Hypothetical life expectancy for given age of regime*

institutions of the old order can be transferred to those of the new order. Whatever symbols are employed in legitimizing the new system, they will have little or no reference to past institutions. At the point where structures become so radically altered that support can no longer be generated for them by invoking the hallowed past, the old regime has ended and a new regime has begun. There would, thus, be a termination of age-related support once this kind of revolutionary change took place. The age-scale counters would be set to zero, and the new regime would have to rely on other means to survive.

Admittedly, there may be instances where it is difficult to apply this criterion, but one should be able to overcome such difficulties. Let us take a look, for example, at the history of France since the Revolution. Obviously the Revolution itself meets our criterion. The overthrow of the revolutionary regime by Napoleon and the establishment of the First Empire undoubtedly constituted another new beginning. Probably the restoration of the Monarchy in 1815 could be considered the start of another distinctly new regime rather than the continuation of the pre-revolutionary regime. How to handle the short-lived Second Republic is problematical. It was obviously a break with the regime that immediately preceded it, but i might have gained some support by invoking the symbols of the First Republic. The Third and the Fourth Republic were interrupted by the Vichy regime, which was clearly something new, but the structural differences between these republics were not very great. While the changes between the Fourth and the Fifth Republic were more significant, one would probably have to conclude that the French "system" has remained essentially intact since the establishment of the Third Republic, and that there has been enough continuity (aside from the Vichy interruption) of some of the institutions (the Chamber of Deputies, for example) despite considerable changes in structure and functions, that we can consider that the system dates from the 1870s.

This covers the suggested ways of operationalizing all of the concepts in our model of the political system. Most attention was directed at institutionalization and responsive capacity because they are the key concepts that would be involved in an empirical evaluation of the legislative system, although, in principle, goal achievement provides the final criterion for such an evaluation. Also in the "path" of the legislative process are social and political differentiation, and some attention will be given these variables.

In Figure 4 the principal concepts concerning the legislative system have been extracted from the overall model, and one of the concepts has been elaborated in more detail. It is this model that we will subject to a test in the following section.

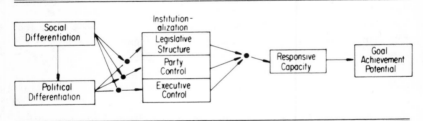

Figure 4. Model of goal-oriented legislative system

## TESTING THE LEGISLATIVE SYSTEM MODEL

### RESPONSIVE CAPACITY

There is still a barrier to surmount before we can actually measure responsive capacity. Because we have determined that it is necessary to use dynamic, change statistics instead of static, cross-sectional statistics, we have three time periods or lags to consider in each observation: that for measuring the change in the need variable, that for measuring the change in the response variable, and that between the measurement of need and of response. Our present purpose is to determine which time periods and lags provide the maximum reliability in the measurement of the need-response relationship. Essentially, the procedure will be to vary the time periods and the lags between them to find the maximum correlation for each set of need-response relationships.

We seek to maximize correlations because we wish to minimize the influences of random or short-term fluctuations and feedback effects on the composition of our index. These would all tend to depress the correlation coefficient. Consequently, we can infer that the time period and lag combination producing the highest correlation would be the one in which these factors were the least involved. Too short a time period for measuring change will tend to be unduly subject to short-term fluctuations and randomness. Political authorities would not be expected to respond systematically to these. A longer time period would tap longer-term trends, but if it were coupled with a short time lag, the need and response periods could overlap so much that part of the variance in the percentage change in need would be a result of change in response. How much overlap we could tolerate before this became a significant factor would depend upon the time that elapsed between the enactment of a policy and its impact on the environment. Presumably, one would want to avoid an overlap equal to or greater than this elapsed time.

Because the combination of a time period and time lag that produced the maximum correlation would define the amount of time necessary for a change in need to be converted to a change in policy, our measure of responsiveness should be one based on this time lag. We would certainly not wish to judge the responsiveness of a system before it had a chance to respond. On the other hand, if we took our measure too long after the response took place, it would be adulterated with response variations related to need changes subsequent to those we recorded. Again, maximizing the correlation between need and response is the best available solution for determining optimum response lag.

It should be noted at this point that, where the maximum correlation between a particular need and a hypothesized response is below a level that would be considered significant by ordinary statistical standards, one ought to reject the hypothesis that this was the correct response to this need. Such evidence suggests, at least, that it is not the typical or customary response by political systems to such conditions and, therefore, one should rethink and reform his hypotheses relating to this area of need. Where there is a substantial correlation, on the other hand, one can be reasonably confident that the coupling of the need and response variables was correct in that the response was perceived as the appropriate one by the authorities in most political systems under the particular conditions of need.

All of the data used in testing our model and in determining optimum time lags and periods are from the American states. It will not be argued, by any means, that these represent a "sample" of world political systems, but it is maintained that their use is justified in the pilot study reported here which seeks only to explore some of the defects and virtures of the proposed model and to assess the practicality of the prescribed method. The means of constructing the various indexes in this study and the method of analysis have been designed so that they would be equally applicable to cross-national studies, and one should be able to apply what is learned here to such studies. U.S. state data have generally been found to have the virtue of convenience and some important research advantages as well. The data are generally more reliable than much of the national data available, and this reliability goes further back in time than it does for most nation-states. This latter becomes a significant consideration in longitudinal analysis.[2] Since measurement of much of the data is done or supervised by the federal government, universal standards are applied across states, and measurement error is minimized. In another sense the states are ideal for comparative analysis because they are similar enough to make them truly comparable, but there is sufficient variance among them in most measures of interest to political scientists to make comparison fruitful.

So much for the virture of the states as arenas for research. Let us see how these data are applied to the problem of determining optimal time periods and lags. For the purpose of simplification, it was first decided to use the same periods of time for measuring change in need and change in response. This may seem somewhat arbitrary, but it is not unreasonable, and if it is not done the number of combinations becomes unmanageable. It was then decided to use three need-response sets in the health, education, and welfare area. The need variable in each instance was measured for the following years: 1958, 1960, 1963, 1964, and 1966. This permitted the construction of the following time periods for measuring change: 2 years (1958-1960), 3 years (1960-1963), 4 years (1960-1964), 5 years (1958-1963), 6 years (1958-1964), and 8 years (1958-1966). The policy or response data were recorded for every year from 1960 through 1971. This permitted the matching of time lags starting at 2 years for each time period up to the total number of years of each particular period, except for the 8-year period where maximum lags could be only 5 years because our data did not go beyond 1971. In this respect, we could have pushed the first year for measuring the need variable back 3 years so that the lags could have been extended to 8 years, but we did not think lags of this length would prove optimal. And for subsequent analytical purposes, it was desirable that our data generally be associated with the 1960s. An example of a time period of 5 years and a lag of 3 years would mean that the change in need was measured from 1958 to 1963, and the response from 1961 to 1966.

The three need-response sets analyzed and their components were as follows:

(1) Welfare. The need variable was change in the number of individuals and family units with income of less than $3,000.[3] Two response variables were used: change in the number of welfare recipients in all categories of welfare, and change in total expenditures on welfare recipients. The correlations were generally higher for the former, so only this variable was used for further analysis.

(2) Education. The need variable was change in the number of children of school age (from 5 to 18 years). The response variable was change in state expenditures to local school districts. It was felt that moderate to heavy increases in the need variable would exacerbate inequities and bring pressures for greater state assistance to the local districts.

(3) Health. The need variable was an aggregation of mortality statistics, including deaths from diseases and all infant deaths. Accidental deaths, suicides, and homicides were excluded. The response variable was change in state expenditures for public health, state hospitals, and Medicaid.

Table 2 presents the product-moment correlation coefficients for the various time periods and lags in the welfare area.

*Table 2. Welfare policy correlations*

| Time Lags, years | Time Periods, years | | | | | |
|---|---|---|---|---|---|---|
| | 2 | 3 | 4 | 5 | 6 | 8 |
| 2 | .10 | .14 | .10 | .22 | .10 | .10 |
| 3 | | .23 | .26 | .35 | .29 | .30 |
| 4 | | | .10 | .38 | .20 | .20 |
| 5 | | | | .21 | .27 | .10 |
| 6 | | | | | .19 | — |

The 5-year time period with the 4-year lag seems to be optimal for measuring responsiveness in this area. Most of the correlations for the 5-year time span for measuring change were higher than corresponding coefficients for other time periods, so it appears that 5 years is about right for smoothing out the rough edges resulting from randomness and short-term fluctuations. The case for selecting a 4-year over a 3-year lag is not very strong, however. Most of the coefficients for a 3-year lag time are higher than those for a 4-year lag, and it is only in the 5-year measurement period that the 4-year lag shows maximum correlation. After taking this and other considerations into account, the 3-year instead of the 4-year lag was selected as optimal.

The "other considerations" just mentioned caused some reexamination of this measurement process. To begin with, one would have expected a very short time lag between the appearance of this need and the change in the number of people on welfare. Surely it does not take 4 years to incorporate newly impoverished or new poor people into the welfare system. This realization prompted an analysis of the feedback effect of the response on the environmental need. The lagging of the variables was reversed, that is, the need variable was measured after the response variable. This could not be done for every period and lag shown in Table 2 because the years for which our need data were collected were not appropriate for this purpose, but it was possible to look at some of the shorter time and lag periods. For the short periods and lags, there was a small but discernible reciprocal or feedback effect. For a 2-year measurement period and a 2-year lag, the correlation was -.27. This is not very large, but it is in the opposite direction from the correlations when the lags are the other way around, which does suggest that there is some tendency for the policy response to reduce the need. Despite the evidence of Table 2, it may be that a 2-year lag, therefore, is a more realistic estimate of how long the actual process takes. When measuring change over a 5-year period, however, a 2-year lag would involve a 3-year overlap of the time periods, which is long enough to incorporate the feedback effect in this measure and thereby depress the correlation coefficient. Going to a 3-year lag and a 2-year overlap probably eliminates it altogether. Unfortunately, by the end of 4 years one would expect considerable attenuation in the response pattern, which would preclude this as an optimum measure of responsiveness. Adopting a short time period for measuring change does not help, because the correlations for these are all much lower than for the 5-year period. Thus, we are forced to compromise between what seems to be the optimum time period and lag combination based on the correlations and what one would realistically consider to be the actual lag in the process. Hence the decision to adopt the 3-year lag and the 5-year period.

The above analysis may slightly lower one's confidence that the matrix of correlation coefficients, by itself, provides evidence on what the actual lag times are. Other less systematic data need to be considered. For further analytical purposes, however, one would not wish to diverge very much from the evidence provided by the correlation matrix, because in doing so he would risk the possibility of lowering the precision of our measuring instrument.

Table 3 shows the correlations for educational policy versus need.

Table 3. *Educational policy correlations*

| Time Lags, years | Time-Periods, years | | | | | |
|---|---|---|---|---|---|---|
| | 2 | 3 | 4 | 5 | 6 | 8 |
| 2 | .01 | .36 | .00 | .34 | .28 | .13 |
| 3 | | –.10 | –.09 | .16 | .15 | .06 |
| 4 | | | –.11 | .09 | .01 | .00 |
| 5 | | | | –.05 | –.03 | .01 |
| 6 | | | | | –.05 | – |

There is little question that the 2-year lag time is optimal for measuring the impact of need on this policy variable, but there is no clear case for either the 3- or the 5-year period for measuring change in the variables. The coefficient for the 3-year period is slightly higher, but does not differ significantly from that for the 5-year period. All things considered, the 5-year period would probably be the best, because the longer periods tend to provide more reliable resutls and in this case there is little danger of incorporating a feedback effect in the 3-year overlap. It is hard to conceive that a change in state school aid would cause a change in the number of school-aged children, at least in the short run.

In table 4, which presents the health policy correlations, we again find that the 5-year period for measuring is the most suitable time period, and in this case a 3-year lag is clearly the optimum.

Table 4. *Health policy correlations*

| Time Lags, years | Time Periods, years | | | | | |
|---|---|---|---|---|---|---|
| | 2 | 3 | 4 | 5 | 6 | 8 |
| 2 | .10 | .15 | .17 | .10 | .12 | .12 |
| 3 | | .16 | .00 | .33 | .09 | .14 |
| 4 | | | .04 | .09 | .12 | .22 |
| 5 | | | | .10 | .12 | .02 |
| 6 | | | | | .00 | – |
| | | | | | .01 | |

It may be observed that even the maximum correlations in each of the areas are not very large; however, they are probably high enough for our initial purposes, that is, for determining optimum time periods and time lags. In using change data of this sort, one expects lower coefficients than would be obtained in straight cross-sectional analysis, primarily because the risk of measurement error is doubled as a result of the fact that there are two observations for each case.[4]

Among the three policy areas, we would have the most confidence that the need-response association in the welfare area was significant. The results here appear to be a little more reliable because of the consistency of the coefficients. About two-thirds of the coefficients would be considered significant with a one-tailed test at the .05 level, and nearly one-half would be at the .01 level. Table 3, on the other hand, shows some negative coefficients, and many in Table 4 are extremely low.

In defining the concepts in our model, it was mentioned that responsive capacity could be considered to have two dimensions, effectiveness and efficiency. Effectiveness is what we have just attempted to measure by means of the residuals from the regression analysis. By efficiency we mean the promptness with which the response is made. In terms of the foregoing analysis, those states with the shortest lag times would be the most efficient. It might be possible to determine the actual response time for each state by graphical methods and with the kind of time-series data we have here, although results obtained in this way would lack precision. We can determine response time a bit more systematically, however, by categorizing states on various bases and then performing the same kind of analysis as was done above to determine optimum lag for each category. This kind of analysis was made on the basis of degrees of institutionalization according to several indicator variables and is described further on.

After settling on the time period for measuring the need and the response variables and on the appropriate time lag between the measurements for each of the three policy areas, I tested the correlation between the resulting residuals and a number of environmental variables to determine which, if any, might be used in "purifying" the responsiveness indexes. The following variables and the indicated policy-area residuals were correlated:

(1)     Per capita income—all three areas.

(2)     Gini coefficient of income maldistribution—welfare policy.

(3)     Index of inequality in expenditures among school districts in the state—education policy.

(4)    Number of physicians in private practice per 10,000 population—health policy.

(5)    Number of private hospital beds per 10,000—health policy.

It was somewhat surprising to find that all of these correlations were rather low, although the correlations of per capita income with all three measures were significant at the .05 level. There was a slight tendency then for the high-income states to be more effective in their responses than the low-income states, so the three indexes were adjusted accordingly by controlling for per capita income.

Referring back to Figure 4, we note that the three independent variables to be employed in the test of the model are social differentiation, political differentiation, and institutionalization. We will use summary or composite indexes for the first two variables, and five separate measures of institutionalization that tap somewhat different dimensions of this concept.

### SOCIAL DIFFERENTIATION

For the single, composite measure of social differentiation, I relied on a measure of "diversity within a population" devised by Lieberson (1969) and computed for the American states by Sullivan (1973). Six demographic, polytomous variables were used, and these were subdivided into a total of 16 categories. These variables and their subdivisions are shown in Table 5.

The index of diversity or heterogeneity, which is designated as $A_w$ is computed by the following formula:

$$A_w = 1 - ( \sum_{k=1}^{p} Y_k^2 / V )$$

where $Y_k$ = the proportion of the population falling in a given category within each of the variables

$V$ = number of variables

$p$ = total number of categories within all of the variables

This is interpretable in probability terms, as it represent the proportion of characteristics upon which a randomly selected pair of individuals will differ (assuming sampling with replacement). That is, if an infinite number of pairs were selected randomly from a finite population, the average proportion of unshared characteristics of these pairs would be $A_w$.

*Table 5. Social and economic variables included in diversity index*

1. Educational Variable:
   - (a)  Less than 5 years of education
   - (b)  More than 5 years of education but did not finish high school
   - (c)  High school education
   - (d)  College education

2. Income Variable:
   - (a)  Families that earn less than $6,000 a year
   - (b)  Families that earn between $6,000 and $10,000 a year
   - (c)  Families that earn over $10,000 a year

3. Occupational Variable:
   - (a)  White-collar occupations
   - (b)  Other occupations

4. Housing Variable:
   - (a)  Home ownership
   - (b)  Renter occupied

5. Ethnic Variable:
   - (a)  Foreign stock
   - (b)  Native stock

6. Religious Variables:
   - (a)  Jewish
   - (b)  Catholic
   - (c)  Protestant and other

As a matter of interest, Table 6 presents the states at both extremes of this measure—the five most heterogeneous states and the five most homogeneous states.

*Table 6. Diversity indexes for ten states*

| | Most Heterogenous | | | Most Homogeneous | |
|---|---|---|---|---|---|
| *Rank* | *State* | *Index Value* | *Rank* | *State* | *Index Value* |
| 1 | New York | .556 | 46 | Tennessee | .346 |
| 2 | Connecticut | .543 | 47 | South Carolina | .345 |
| 3 | Massassachusetts | .541 | 48 | North Carolina | .342 |
| 4 | New Jersey | .538 | 49 | Arkansas | .333 |
| 5 | Hawaii | .528 | 50 | Mississippi | .330 |

## POLITICAL DIFFERENTIATION

It should be recalled that political differentiation of the legislative system as conceived here is characterized by the importance and autonomy of the legislative function and by a functional diversity within the system. The approach to measuring political differentiation was to select three variables that appeared to tap the three dimensions of the concept and combine them in a composite score. The following variables (which are measured for the 1963-64 legislative sessions) were considered to be related to the importance, autonomy, and diversity of the legislative system:

(1)  Compensation of legislators. This is essentially a measure of autonomy and indirectly a measure of importance. The more autonomous legislatures will be less constrained to set legislative salaries at a high level. Also, the more active legislatures will require a greater amount of time on the part of legislators, and consequently there will be greater motivation and justification for higher salaries.

(2)  Number of enactments per biennium. This is an indicator of the activity and importance of the legislative function. It should also tend to reflect to some degree political diversity.

(3)  Number of standing committees in both houses. This is regarded as a measure of diversity, although it is recognized that a large number of committees might tend to diminish rationality in the system.

These three variables combined as a composite and treated individually were correlated with social differentiation, and it was found that compensation of legislators was correlated at a substantially higher level than the other two variables or the combination. Consequently, it was used in the final analysis as a single variable to represent political differentiation.

### INSTITUTIONALIZATION

The concept of institutionalization, it will be recalled, characterizes political structures that are open to communication and the free flow of information and that are rationalized in their decisional processes. The discussion in the previous section on operationalizing institutionalization suggested a rather large number of measures for this concept. It will not be possible in the limited pilot study to follow up on many of these because some of them require quite extensive observations in individual states. A major objective of planned future research is to construct some of these other indexes of institutionalization. For the present study five indicator variables that were assumed to tap significant dimensions of this concept and were available for the time period we were considering (the early 1960s) were selected. These variables are discussed in the following paragraphs.

(1) *Equality of apportionment of legislative districts.* This was considered to be a major indicator of system rationalization. The time period we are concerned with here is just before state legislatures were ordered to be reapportioned by the U.S. Supreme Court, when there existed a large variance in the equity of the approtionment among the states. Among the various measures available, the David-Eisenberg (1961) "index of devaluation of the vote" was deemed the best overall indicator of malapportionment in the context of our conception of institutionalization. In order to have a positive relationship with this concept, the mathematical complement of the index was used.

(2) *Expenditures for legislative research and informational agencies.* The support for such agencies should be a good indicator of both the openness of the legislative system, in that they augment the channels of communication and provide for increased information flow into the system, and of the rationality of the system, in that they provide the means for analyzing policy in terms of the need for it and of the consequences of alternative politics.

(3) *Turnover of legislators.* This is injected into the analysis with a high degree of tentativeness. It is not certain whether this is a measure of institutionalization or the lack of it, but it still seemed worht testing. Our hypothesis is that it is postiively related to institutionalization.

(4) *Total length of legislative sessions per biennium.* This possibly can be considered a measure of system rationality, since the short, infrequent sessions imposed in some states do not provide sufficient time for rational consideration of most legislation. Longer sessions would not guarantee rationality, but they would seem to be a necessary condition for it.

(5) *Index of party competition (the percentage of seats held by the minority party multiplied by 2 and averaged for both houses).* This is

presumed to be interactive with the degree-of-party-control variables listed below. The interaction would be such that party competition would enhance institutionalization when party control is great, but have no effect on it when party control is minimal. The assumption underlying the use of this measure is that, where the level of party competition is high, the parties will be more open to a wide range of members, to information about the problems of society, and to the wishes and demands of the mass electorate. This, of course, really goes back to V. O. Key's now-famous proposition that party competition fostered a desire on the part of party leadership to promote measures beneficial to the majority rather than to the elite.

We have noted previously that the effects of variations in strictly legislative structures relating to an elected assembly may be mediated by variations in the degree of political party or executive control. It was argued that, where such control is significant, the arena of the legislative function is removed to a degree outside the structural confines of the elected assembly. The following measures of party and gubernatorial control were therefore obtained so that they could be tested for interaction with the five institutionalization variables listed above:

(1) *Degree of party control.* Probably the most valid measure of this would be party cohesion scores computed from roll-call votes. To gather the date for such a measure in all states represents a task far greater than can be considered for the present study, so the following surrogate measures were used:

(a) Weber's party professionalism index. This was devised by Ronald Weber.[5] It is simply the percentage of state employees who are not on the state merit system, that is, roughly the proportion of patronage positions. It appears to be a fairly valid indicator of party organizational strength, which, in turn, is a factor in party control and cohesion in the legislature. Furthermore, a comparison of scattered cohesion scores from 12 states obtained from Jewell and Patterson (1973: 445-446) showed that this index predicted these scores rather accurately.

(b) Francis's index of party conflict. Wayne Francis (1968) rated all state legislatures on the level of party conflict or the extent to which the parties took opposing sides on major issues and the degree to which they held their ranks in so doing. The index is based on questionnaires filled out by legislators and is, consequently, somewhat subjective, but it also predicts fairly well the level of cohesion found in the Jewell-Patterson data.

(2)    *Degree of gubernatorial influence and control.* Again, one would have liked a behavioral indicator of this, but such is not available, and one has to resort to the following measures.[6]

(a)    Schlesinger's index of governor's veto powers. Devised by Joseph Schlesinger (1964), this measure was considered the most appropriate of the legalistic indicators because it bears directly on the governor's ability to exercise some control over legislation. It is realized that the correlation between potential power and actual power may not be unity, but one would expect that it would be rather high.

(b)    Governor's electoral margin. This is the percentage of the two-party voted received by the incumbent governor in the previous election (to fit with the legislative data, the elections of either 1960 or 1962). It was assumed that the larger the majority, the greater the tendency of the governor to exercise control over the legislative branch.

The political party and gubernatorial support scores were employed individually in the analysis rather than being combined into a single index of two indexes.

## RESULTS OF ANALYSIS

### THE DETERMINANTS OF RESPONSIVE EFFECTIVENESS

The measured variables were subjected to a multistage, multiple regression analysis as a means of testing the hypothesized relationships among them. The following regression equations were computed:

$$X_2 = a_2 + b_{21}X_1 + c_2 \tag{1}$$

$$X_3 = a_3 + b_{31}X_1 + c_3 \tag{2}$$

$$X_4 = a_4 + b_{41.26}X_1 + b_{42.16}X_2 + b_{46.12}(X_2/X_1) + c_4 \tag{3}$$

$$X_5 = a_5 + b_{51.23467}X_1 + b_{52.13467}X_2 + b_{53.12467}X_3 \tag{4}$$
$$+ b_{54.12367}X_4 + b_{56.12347}(X_2/X_1) + b_{57.12346}(X_4/X_3)$$
$$+ c_5$$

where:

$a$ = intercept value

$b$ = regression coefficient

$c$ = error term

$X_1$ = social differentiation

$X_2$ = political differentiation

$X_3$ = four individual party and gubernatorial control variables

$X_4$ = five individual legislative structure variables

$X_5$ = three individual responsiveness indicators

$(X_2/X_1)$ = interaction factor between political differentiation and social differentiation

$(X_4/X_3)$ = interaction factor between legislative structure variables and party and gubernatorial control variables.[7]

It should be noted that equation 2 is really four separate equations, because four separate variables are successively substituted for $X_3$; that equation 3 is five separate equations representing each of the five structural variables; that equation 4 is three separate equations since each of the responsiveness indicators becomes the dependent variable; that the fourth and fifth terms in equation 4 represent four and five terms (the four variables of $X_3$ and the five variables of $X_4$), respectively; and, finally, that the seventh term in this equation represents 20 individual interactive terms.

The results of this analysis are shown in Figure 5. The standard errors of the individual regression coefficients were computed; and where these were greater than .50 times the regression coefficient, the null hypothesis was accepted and no arrow was drawn connecting the two variables.[8] The values shown above each line are beta coefficients (standardized regression coefficients) and can be regarded as equivalent to path coefficients.

The principal negative finding from this test was that social and political differentiation did not have the combined effect on institutionalization that was hypothesized. The theoretical discussion had put forth the notion that it was not the absolute level of political differentiation that determined the degree of institutionalization but the level in relationship to the development of social differentiation. The interactive term, $b_{46.12}(X_2/X_1)$, was introduced into equation 3 to represent one possible form of the combined effect, that is, one in which the ratio between political and social differentiation would be linearly related to institutionalization. But in none of the applications of equation 3 did $X_2/X_1$

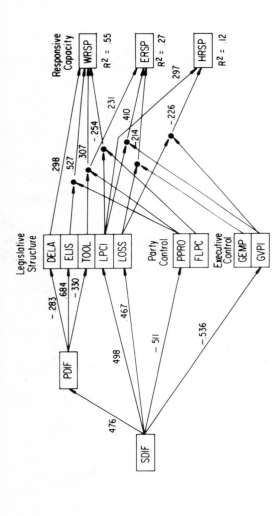

The following code names identify the variables:

SDIF = social differentiation
PDIF = political differentiation
DELA = David-Eisenberg legislative apportionment index
ELIS = expenditures for legislative informational services
TOOL = turnover of legislators
LPCI = legislative party competition index
LOSS = length of legislative sessions

PPRO = party professionalism index
FLPC = Francis's legislative party conflict scores
GEMP = governor's electoral margin percentage
GVPI = governor's veto power index
ERSP = education policy responsiveness
WRSP = welfare policy responsiveness
HRSP = health policy responsiveness

Figure 5. Interrelationships among legislative system variables

account for enough variance in the institutionalization variables to regard this as significant. If the relationship had been one in which the mathematical difference between the two types of differentiation was linearly related to institutionalization, the causal model would have been as follows:

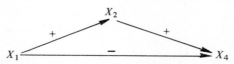

Here the upper path represents a developmental sequence where social differentiation affects institutionalization positively and indirectly through the mediation of political differentiation; while the lower path is the partial, direct effect with political differentiation held constant, and is negative. As may be seen from Figure 5, this did not prove to be true either.

There are a number of interpretations of these results. One possibility is that the effects on institutionalization were actually interactive, but of a different form than specified here. Our initial assumption was that the interaction was in the form of a ratio that varied according to the relative sizes of $X_1$ and $X_2$; thus, as political differentiation lagged more and more behind social differentiation, the ratio got smaller and smaller. It is conceivable that the form might have been exponential, such as $X_2^{-X_1}$, although this did not seem as plausible at first, or it might be represented by some complicated polynomial. Only further testing of other models could show which.

The scale for measuring these two variables is also critical. In order to make them as similar as possible, the values for both were converted to standard scores, and because the ratio was not supposed to exceed +1, they were further adjusted to eliminate the few instances where it did. But this is all rather arbitrary. It forces the variables to have the same mean and standard deviation. Whereas this procedure might be difficult to justify, the adjustment to eliminate ratios greater than unity is even more difficult to defend. Still, at this state of the art one has to try and see what works.

Another explanation for the results is that the indicator variables were not measuring what they were intended to measure. Here one does what seems reasonable. I have some confidence in the social differentiation (SDIF) variable, a little less in the political differentiation (PDIF) variable, and think that possibly two of the institutionalization variables, legislative party competition index (LPCI) and length of legislative sessions (LOSS), might be moved back to become part of the political differentiation measure. Notice that their correlation with SDIF is about the same as that of the political differentiation index with SDIF and that PDIF does not mediate the effects of SDIF on them. There are some logical reasons for combining these two into a new PDIF indicator. Although the existence of party competition in the legislature might not always be an indication of political differentiation, we are fairly certain that the opposite condition, one-party control, is a good indication of the lack of it. And the notion that LPCI is an *indicator* of openness in the system is probably not as sound as the notion that it may be a *cause* of openness in the system; therefore, it belongs at this prior stage in the model. LOSS is in some sense similar to compensation of legislators in that it is likely to reflect, in part, the importance attached to the legislative function and the autonomy of the legislative system with respect to its ability to decide how long it should meet.

Finally, the analysis might have been slightly adulterated by the size dimension creeping into some of the variables. For example, one can conceive of the possibility of spuriousness resulting from the fact that the larger states tend to be more differentiated both socially and politically and that they would also tend to spend more money on such things as legislative information services. Normally, in comparative analyses of this sort, one converts expenditures figures into per capita amounts. Such a conversion was not made in this study because the legislature was regarded as a unit with certain necessary costs regardless of the population of the state. To be equally informed, a legislature in Alaska would require legislative information services of almost the same size and quality as those required by the legislature of the state of New York. But size is not totally irrelevant. There is a sense in which there is more "information" to be gathered and processed in a large state as compared to a small one. The problem is to find or devise a "size" function to apply to these expenditures to adjust them to the varying effects of population size. I think it is clear, however, that a straight division by population is not the right function.

In view of the several plausible alternative explanations, we would have little basis for rejecting the notion that institutionalization is related to social and political differentiation in either the interactive or additive manner described above, but we are, of course, provided with no basis for accepting it either. Further work in this area should help to clarify the issue. This pilot study has pointed up some of the possible operational and analytical defects in the initial formulation of this problem, and that is as far as we can hope to go at this time.

With respect to the effect of political differentiation on the five indicators of institutionalization, in only one instance is the association significant and in the hypothesized direction, that is, the association with expenditures for legislative informational services. This is fairly substantial, and a look at individual examples suggests that the population size factor is not involved in producing a spurious correlation. The signs for the other two paths—to David-Eisenberg legislative apportionment index (DELA) and turnover of legislators (TOOL)—are negative, which is cause for rejection of our initial hypothesis. These latter results are really inexplicable in terms of our theory, but it is interesting to speculate about the reasons for them. In the first case the implication is that the equitability of legislative apportionment suffers with an increase in political differentiation. The reason might be seen in the fact that it is almost always in the interest of incumbent legislators to avoid a reapportionment, and where they are autonomous (politically differentiated) this unpleasantry is more easily avoided. Because these measurements were taken before Baker vs. Carr, this event would have to be regarded as causing a general reduction in autonomy for all state legislative bodies in the United States.

The negative sign on the path to TOOL would seem to be consistent with Huntington's and Polsby's thinking that members of autonomous institutions tend to put a high value on their institutional roles and make it difficult for other contenders to dislodge them.[9] They may be correct in this assumption, but in going the next step in the analysis we note that the effects of variations in turnover are in the direction hypothesized and not in the generally assumed direction. A high rate of turnover contributes to greater responsiveness, at least in the welfare and educational policy areas. It seems quite reasonable to believe that systems with high turnover rates would be more open in the sense that I have defined this as a characteristic of institutionalization. They could very well be more flexible, adaptable, and more open to a wide variety of solutions to problems. In the theoretical phase of this study, an attempt was made to distinguish clearly between political differentiation and institutionalization and to define the latter in such a way as to move it into closer association with responsive capacity by incorporating into this definition those structural characteristics that seemed the most conducive to responsive capacity. In the operationalizing of these concepts, then, this scheme seems to have been carried out with some success. If political differentiation and the institutionalization variables had not been so clearly differentiated, there would have been consistently high positive coefficients on the connecting paths between these sets of variables. The fact that such coefficients were not obtained suggests that the two concepts are distinct, should be analyzed separately, and are not part of a "development syndrome," as one author has put it (Binder, 1971: 21, 22). On the other hand, the institutionalization variables turned out to be rather closely associated with responsiveness and generally in the direction predicted. At least as a group they were much more closely associated than was political differentiation. Equation 4 provided the test for this, and in none of its versions was the coefficient for PDIF considered large enough to be significant. It is true that this was never coupled with the party or gubernatorial control variables in the regression analysis, but the simple correlation coefficients between it and the responsiveness variables were so low (and nenegative in the case of welfare policy responsiveness, WRSP) that it appeared highly unlikely that interaction with any of the "control" variables would have made any difference. It seems improbable, then, that, had we adopted some of the previous concepts of institutionalization that relied heavily on the notion of autonomy, we would have found any substantial connection with responsive capacity.

In a very important respect the model tested out as predicted. This was in regard to the interactive effects of the party and gubernatorial control variables with the institutionalization variables. In only two instances was there a direct association between the latter and any of the responsiveness indexes. One of these involved the direct relationship between legislative apportionment and welfare responsiveness. This was the only effect of apportionment that was detected, and it was not very substantial. This finding seems to be in accord with most of the studies of legislative reapportionment in the American states, which have found the effects rather elusive or barely detectable (see especially Patterson, 1971; Hofferbert, 1966). One possible reason variations in these control variables did not appear to affect this relationship may be that an equitably apportioned legislature has a certain aura of legitimacy about it that may make it somewhat more immune to actual control by party leaders or the executive, even where the potential for control is high. As the reader will recall, our control measures are unfortunately indicative of potential rather than actual control. The other example of direct effect is the relationship between party competition and health policy responsiveness, which we will touch upon shortly.

Outside of these two examples, however, the relationships of the structural variables with the responsiveness variables were affected by the level of political control in at least one of its four dimensions. We can draw this interpretation from the fact that more of the variance was explained in the dependent variables by the interaction factors than by the straight linear correlation with each of these four structural variables. When welfare responsiveness was being measured, the party control variables significantly interacted with the structural variables, whereas executive control variables were involved in the interaction where educational and health responsiveness were being assessed. The explanation for the welfare responsiveness example must be that welfare issues tend to engender more partisan conflict than issues in the other two areas, and thereby enhance the probability that the potential for party control will become actual. Where this is true, high values of the structural variables will not be associated necessarily with high values of the responsiveness variable because the arena of decision making has shifted toward the party. Hence, a given level of correlation between the structural and responsiveness variables will be augmented by adjusting the former according to variations in the level of political party control, in this instance through the process of dividing the structural score by the party control score. By the same reasoning, the interactive influence of executive control variables in the education and health fields suggests greater concern or ability of the governor than of party leaders (should there be a difference) in exerting influence on these kinds of issues.

A finding that seems to diverge from the theory is seen in the negative effect of the interaction between LPCI and Francis's legislative party conflict scores (FLPC) on the welfare policy variable. In seeking an explanation for this effect, let us first note that legislative competition was assumed to enhance responsiveness only where party control was relatively strong and would have little influence where the control was weak. Consequently, a multiplicative interaction was hypothesized for these two variables, whereas for the other four structural indicators, the interaction was expressed as a quotient. This negative path, therefore, seems to indicate that where party competition and control are high, responsiveness tends to be low, and where the former are low, the latter is high. But closer analysis suggests that the finding is not so much in contradiction to the theory as one that was simply not encompassed by the theory. Another look at the Francis legislative partisan conflict index shows that it is actually what its label says it is and cannot be assumed to be a measure of party strength as I proposed. It is rather highly correlated with party competition ($r = +.80$) and is not correlated at all with the other alleged indicator of party strength or control, the party professionalism index. Party competition by itself is slightly correlated negatively with WRSP, but this negative correlation increases when it is combined multiplicatively with FPCI. In view of these additional facts, it then appears that a high level of party competition tends to reduce the capacity of the system to respond to welfare needs because it is more difficult for the majority party to get a majority vote in the legislature on welfare bills, since by definition, the majority party's majority is very slim when competition is high. This condition is apparently exacerbated when a high level of competition is combined with a high degree of party conflict in the legislature. Probably, the latter condition makes it more difficult to compromise and gain the majorities needed for passage. This seems to add another nail in the coffin of V. O. Key's theory about party competition and welfare legislation.

The small positive effect of party competition on health policy is not in accord with our theory because it is unaffected by the political control variables, but it also seems to be in conflict with the above findings. Additional policy areas must be analyzed to shed more light on this effect, but one might conclude that party competition was actually a good indicator of the openness of the system and would generally lead to greater responsiveness except in those policy areas where partisan conflict was highly salient. Party competition can make legislators more alert to needs of constituents and at least give them the motivation, if not the conditions, for responding to these needs. Health policy probably is not an area that engenders much party conflict, and thus the barriers to compromise on legislation in this field resulting from such conflict are not very high. This would explain the lack of interaction with the partisan conflict variable. And, if health policy engenders little party conflict, one would also expect to find little party voting on health issues. So party strength or cohesion would have little relevance in this area, which should explain why there was also no interaction with the other party "control" variable, the party professionalism index.

The impact of party competition on educational policy responsive capacity is somewhat more consistent with our theory. The moderate positive coefficient for the interactive path indicates that this area of responsive capacity will tend to be high when competition is intense and the governor's power potential is low. This evidence therefore provides some further support for our initial notion that party competition contributes to the openness of the system. It is not in accord with our original assumption, however, that its effects on responsiveness are interactive with the degree of party control, and the reasons are probably the same as just indicated with regard to health policy. That is to say, the parties are probably more divided among themselves on education than on welfare issues, for example, and little actual party control is exercised on these. On the other hand, the interaction with the gubernatorial control variable suggests that these issues are ones on which the executive might frequently take a stand and would tend to exert his power over the legislature.

Finally, the effects of length of session on responsiveness were not very close to what was predicted, even though an interactive effect was apparently involved. From the path analysis the indication is that responsiveness decreases (in both the health and welfare areas) with an increase in session length and with a low level of executive control. There is no readily available explanation for this decrease. It is hard to believe that the legislatures with short, infrequent sessions would tend to be more responsive in any respects than those that met more regularly and were less rushed in pursuing the legislative function. The relatively low value of the coefficients, coupled with the lack of a plausible explanation for the negative sign, suggests that this result is simply a "fluke."

The negative results with respect to length of session as well as party competition also point up a possible weakness in the method used. The use of ratio or multiplicative terms to represent the sort of interaction that was hypothesized was an expedient. These could express only partially the kind of interaction I had in mind, which was a situation where one variable determines the degree of association of two other variables. Probably the most acceptable way of testing for this condition is to partition the covariance of the latter two variables according to intervals of the former and then to employ analysis of covariance to determine if there is significant difference in covariance among the categories established by the partitioning variable. The difficulty with this approach is that it is not compatible with the multiple-regression approach used in testing the rest of the model. It is very convenient to assume a ratio or multiplicative form of interaction and simply enter the quotient or product as another variable in a multiple regression equation. And, generally, this should approximate rather well the form of the relationship. If, for example, a high value of a third variable causes an increase in the covariance of two other variables, then adjusting the independent variable of the latter set by multiplying by the values of the third variable has the effect of increasing its variance in categories of cases where the covariance with the dependent variable is high and decreasing its variance where the covariance is low. This, in the aggregate, produces a higher correlation coefficient than that between the unaltered independent variable and the dependent. Thus, one might reasonably regard a significant difference between the two coefficients as evidence of the hypothesized interaction. One encounters some difficulties with this method, however, if the third variable is significantly correlated with the dependent variable. When the simple correlations involved are positive, multiplying the independent by the third variable will produce a higher correlation than the initial one even when there is no interaction. This is apparently not a difficulty with the other four structural variables, but it does seem to affect the analysis of the fifth one (length of legislative sessions) and the two hypothesized interactive variables (the governor's veto power index and vote margin). The correlations of the latter with the two responsive capacity variables, although they were quite low, nevertheless make the findings with regard to the effects of length of sessions virtually uninterpretable. The remedy for this situation might have been to factor out the variance in the dependent variable attributable to the four political control variables before proceeding with the analysis. In this study it was not done because the relevant correlations were so low and the process was considered to have an unduly complicating effect on the analysis.[10]

The coefficients of multiple determination shown below the three dependent variables in Figure 5 suggest that the effects of institutionalization are the greatest in the welfare policy field. Four of the five structural variables have an impact on this and account for 55 percent of the variance in welfare responsive capacity. Education responsiveness comes next with three structural variables accounting for 27 percent of the variance in this index. In the health policy field, only two variables have a significant impact, and these account for only 12 percent of the variance in responsiveness. It is not surprising that welfare issues tend to be sensitive to structural variations. They often generate a good deal of conflict and close divisions within American state legislatures. A structural change that would give a slight advantage to one coalition as against another would have a greater tendency to affect legislative output than where divisions were not so sharp. Furthermore, it appears that there is slightly more executive involvement in educational and health policy matters than in welfare; and although we have tried to account for or adjust for this by means of the interactive factors, if such influence is consistently higher in one policy area than another, this will tend to diminish the impact of structural variation on responsive capacity. Finally, the differences noted in the three fields might be explainable to some degree by the seemingly greater reliability of the welfare responsiveness index. In the discussion of the construction of this index it was noted that the pattern and consistency of the correlations for the various time periods and time lags pointed to the greater reliability of this index over the other two. Obviously, if there is more measurement error involved in the health and education indexes, measures of association of these with other variables will tend to be diminished.

In order to gain an additional perspective on how significant were the effects of structural variation on responsive capacity, a "dummy" variable representing whether the legislature was controlled by the Democrats or the Republicans, or whether the two houses were split between the two parties was included among the structural variables ($X_4$) in equation 4. While the Democratic-controlled legislatures tended to be more responsive than the other two types, especially where party strength was high and especially in the welfare policy field, in each field two or more of the structural variables accounted for more of the variance in responsiveness than the type of party control. Some of the implications of this finding are rather interesting as it suggests that a change in certain structural characteristics will tend to affect responsiveness more than a change in the control from one party to another. It further suggests that the voters cannot exercise very much influence over the policy output of the system by means of the ballot box. Those dissatisfied with the responsiveness of the system might do better to work for a constitutional convention to alter the structure of the legislative institution.

## THE DETERMINANTS OF RESPONSIVE EFFICIENCY

The major analysis presented in this paper is focused on the effects of institutionalization and the *effectiveness* of legislative response in three policy areas. A smaller, less complicated study was undertaken concurrently to determine the effects of the structural variables related to insittutionalization on the *efficiency* of response. The reader will recall that this was defined as the rapidity with which the system converted needs to responses. Four of the five structural variables—DELA, expenditures for legislative informational services (ELIS), TOOL, and LOSS— were dichotomized at the mean, which created for each variable two gropus of states, those with the most institutionalization structures and those with the least. Purely for convenience, we will refer to the former as "reformed" systems and the latter as "unreformed." Then the optimum time lag for each group of states and for each of the three policy areas was computed and compared. The hypothesis was that the reformed states would be more efficient, that is, that they would show a shorter optimum time lag between measurement of need and response.

The results generally confirmed the hypothesis, though they were mixed. Expenditures for legislative informational services and equitability of approtionment seemed generally to have the most effect, particularly the former on welfare policy and the latter on educational policy response. We will take a closer look at these two particular cases.

Expenditures for informational services had a highly skewed distribution, and when these were divided at the mean, there were 10 systems above (reformed) and 38 systems below (unreformed). The 5-year period for measuring change was used throughout, and correlations were computed for each set of legislative systems, for lag times of 2, 3, 4, and 5 years, and for each of the need-response areas. Table 7 shows the marked difference in optimum response times in the welfare policy area. This suggests very strongly that response time in the reformed states was two years shorter than that in the unreformed states.

It is also interesting to examine the regression equations for the

## Table 7. Welfare policy correlations

| | Time Lags, years | | | |
|---|---|---|---|---|
| | 2 | 3 | 4 | 5 |
| High-expenditure states | .83 | .68 | .48 | .32 |
| Low-expenditure states | .19 | .25 | .32 | .14 |

two sets of states for a 2-year response time. For the high-expenditure states, it is as follows:

$$X_R = .01 + .46X_N$$

where

$X_R$ = estimated value of response

$X_N$ = value of need

For the remaining states, the equation is:

$$X_R = -.10 + .08X_N$$

It can be seen by comparing these equations that the response, on the average, is of a greater magnitude in the reformed states and is consistently so, since the regression line for these states starts off at a higher level and climbs more steeply as need increases.

The second case involved the equitability of the apportionment of legislative districts. According to this, there were 22 in the reformed category (equitably apportioned) and 26 in the unreformed. Table 8 shows the correlations for the various lag times for each set of states in the education policy field.

## Table 8. Education policy correlations

| | Time Lags, years | | | |
|---|---|---|---|---|
| | 2 | 3 | 4 | 5 |
| Equitably apportioned states | .52 | .15 | -.08 | -.19 |
| Malapportioned states | .18 | .17 | .42 | .25 |

Again, the reformed states show a faster response (2 years) than the unreformed (4 years).

These two cases show that there are some rather high correlations for subsets of states that are presumably more homogeneous in regard to response time. This should renew our confidence in the reliability of the need-response combinations as measures of responsiveness. A reason for the fairly low coefficients resulting from correlating all 48 states is that they have varying response times, and the ones whose time does not correspond to a particular time-lag category will tend to depress the overall correlation coefficient for that category. This seems to argue for treating each legislative system differently in regard to response time and for each policy area. If we want separate measures of efficiency and effectiveness, we should not let the former corrupt the latter. This is what happens if we measure effectiveness for all states at the same response time. We would need, therefore, to determine the optimum response time for each state. This would make construction of the responsiveness index much more complicated, and it might not be worth the effort in terms of more reliable results, but it could be accomplished. One approach might be to use some form of discriminant analysis that would identify the optimal grouping of states within time-lag categories to maximize the average correlations with the categories.

## CONCLUSIONS

The pilot study presented here has been useful, I think, in two respects. It has provided a very tentative and partial test of our systems model, but through it we have gained some insights into the strengths and weaknesses of the theory behind the model. And, second, it was useful in exposing some of the defects in the method and in pointing to means of improving it.

The major theoretical conclusion is that institutionalization, as herein defined, tends to have an impact on responsiveness. We cannot assert that this is generally true because the relationship was only apparent for specific conditions and specific areas of policy, but the study strongly affirms that it would be fruitful to pursue the analysis into other areas of public policy and in other political systems. Eventually, we should be able to produce a general index of responsive capacity which could be analyzed together with somewhat more refined measures of institutionalization.

Also of theoretical importance was confirmation that the distinction between institutionalization and political differentiation was a meaningful one and that the two concepts ought not to be combined analytically or be regarded as different dimensions of the same concept. That is to say, there are a number of structural characteristics that contribute to the autonomy of the legislative system and to functional differentiation within that system, and these are not the same as, nor are they necessarily related to, those characteristics that promote openness and foster system rationality. It was, in fact, hypothesized that the two types of characteristics would be related, that political differentiation, to the extent that it kept pace with social differentiation, would provide a basis for institutionalization. But this revision of a more conventional theory about institutionalization was not very strongly supported by the empirical evidence. To avoid a "modernist" bias and to foster the notion that less complex and more traditional societies can be just as responsive as modern, highly differentiated societies, the formulation proposed here was that it was the *gap* between social and political differentiation that made the difference in institutionalization, not the *absolute level* of the latter. The data presented here do not support this notion, so we will have to wait for a more comprehensive analysis to determine whether this proposition is correct.

Another finding of some theoretical importance was that the impact of structural variation on responsiveness is affected by the degree of control over the legislative function exercised by the executive or by party leaders. This generally was supportive of initial hypotheses on this subject. There is apparently some substance to the reasoning that executive or party control shifts the arena of decision making away from the elected assemblies and renders their institutional arrangement irrelevant to those decisions. Previous studies that had shown no or very weak relationships between legislative structures and outputs had failed to consider that such an interactive relationship might be involved. The implications of these findings to those who are interested in "improving" or "reforming" legislative institutions to make them more responsive should be obvious. If it is not, let me pass on the advice that they should concentrate on those systems where gubernatorial and party control are rather weak, at least if they are only interested in making changes in the structures and process of elected assemblies. If they wish to adopt a broader perspective, they should approach those systems where either the governor's or the parties' control is strong and pursue measures that would enhance the openness or rationality of these structures in their role in the legislative process.

A final matter of theoretic significance was seen in the finding that the interactive effects of the party and executive control variables varied across policy areas. The interpretation given to this was that interaction with the party control variable would be characteristic of those policy areas where the issues have a tendency to create strong partisan divisions among legislators, and interaction with executive control variables would take place in policy areas where the executive took a strong stand and a clear position on the issues. Roughly speaking, the welfare area provides an example of the former, and the education and health areas, examples of the latter. If this interpretation is correct, the hypotheses regarding interaction should be refined to include a third dimension: the degree to which variations in the structures of legislative bodies affect the responsiveness of the legislative system is dependent upon the absence of party and executive control of the legislative process, and these effects will diminish generally as control from either or both sources increases generally; but in specific areas of low saliency for either the party or the executive, an increase in general control from the respective source will not diminish such effects.

Now, with respect to methodological conclusions, the major one is that a more dynamic analysis would have been better than the cross-sectional method ecmployed here. This conclusion is not so much derived from the empirical findings of this study as from a persistent conviction, which remained unaltered by the actual analysis, that using change data rather than static data would be a more valid approach to the testing of this model. Change data were not used because their use would have meant gathering at least twice as much data and would have made a complicated analytical process even more complicated. However, a dynamic analysis can and should be done eventually. Such an analysis is superior because one cannot, without a great deal of risk, make inferences about causation when using static, cross-sectional data, at least in reference to the kind of model employed here. Such a multistage model realistically involves a number of time periods: all of the action does not take place simultaneously. If the variations in one variable are postulated as "causing" some of the variability in another variable, one has to assume that the former variation took place at a time before the latter. At the very least, such analysis calls for the measuring of causally prior variables at an earlier time period than the variables they are alleged to affect. But true dynamic analysis requires more than this, and we have to go one step further to rule out the possibility that the direction of causation was the opposite from the assumed. Even though variable A was measured before variable B, it would still be possible that a significant correlation between them could result from variations in B causing variations in A. In particular, this could be true if the values of B changed very slowly over time, which would mean that measurements of B at any two points in time would be highly correlated. Then if a condition of B prior to the measurement of A was responsible for variations in A, A would be correlated with the later measurement of B because of the high correlation between the two measurements of B. We faced this problem earlier in this paper in discussing how to construct the responsive capacity index and determined that the only way around it was to measure *changes* in each of the variables, and measure such change in hypothesized causes before hypothesized effects. A change in one variable occurring before a change in another variable could hardly be considered to have been caused by the latter change.[11]

Even though the responsive capacity indexes are measured with dynamic data, the results are static statistics because they represent a condition at one point in time. In a thoroughly dynamic analysis, we would have to measure change in responsive capacity which would require that we measure the need variable at four separate points in time and the same for the response variable. Figure 6 depicts how this might be done and shows how a structural variable might be measured in terms of time periods so as to be properly time oriented for the analysis.

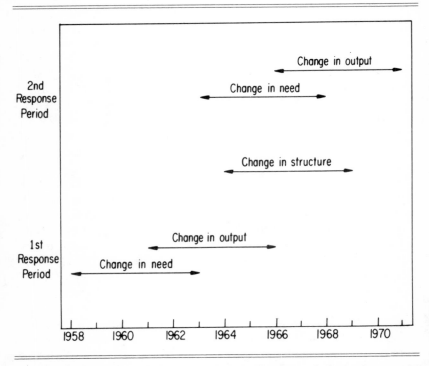

*Figure 6. Time periods for measuring responsiveness and change in structure*

The time periods for measuring change have been set at 5 years for all variables because this seems to be about the optimum period for the empirical data examined so far. A 3-year lag is indicated for a response to be made to a changed condition of need. Again, the findings reported here suggest that this time lag will serve well for most policy areas. The measurement of change in need for the second response period starts where this measurement for the first period ends. Probably, this is as close together as the two periods should be. The measurement of change in structure is inserted somewhat arbitrarily between the two response periods. This particular positioning is based on the assumption that structural changes will take approximately 2 years to affect the level of responsiveness. Thus, we start the measurement of the structural change in 1964, or 2 years before the first response period ends. We terminate it in 1969, 2 years before the second response period ends, as any changes in structure recorded after 1969 would not affect the responsiveness in this second period.

What is being proposed here is simply a quasi-experimental technique that approximates a "before-and-after" study. We measure the responsiveness before changing the legislative structure; then we statistically manipulate the structure and measure the responsiveness again after the manipulation.

In this scheme the measurement of political "control" will be static because the assumption is that the actual level of party or executive control, not a change in this level, will determine how much a change in structure affects responsiveness.

It can be expected that some of the other methodological problems encountered in the pilot study will be resolved or diminished by employing the dynamic approach. For instance, it would seem most unlikely that any of the political control variables would be correlated with change in responsiveness, although we have noted that some are slightly correlated with static level of responsiveness. The suggestion that we would have to partial out the effects of these variables on responsiveness before testing for interaction would probably not need to be followed if the dynamic approach were used. Experience with this method, which is a kind of combination of longitudinal and cross-sectional analysis, indicates that the problem of spuriousness crops up less often than with a straight longitudinal or stright cross-sectional analysis. Some potential causes of spuriousness with the latter two methods that are time-related are partialed out if they affect all units in the same way (e.g., an increase in inflation), while others that are relatively static could not be expected to be correlated with changes in experimental variables.

The final appraisal of our pilot study will have to be that it represents only a stage in the development of a more thorough and comprehensive testing of the theoretical model presented here. As indicated, the findings can be regarded only as very tentative, but the study did demonstrate that the concepts in the model could be operationalized in a reasonable manner and that the hypothetical connections between them could be tested. The operationlizing and measuring of some of the concepts were undoubtedly rather crude, but the study showed that some indicators are better than others and provided some guidance as to where additional work should be done.

Another fundamental limitation of the pilot study was that it dealt exclusively with systems where the legislative function was presumed to be dominated by typically constituted legislative bodies. The conception of the legislative system offered in the first part of this essay allows for the possibility of the legislative function being dominated by executive structures or political parties; but the study has provided no direct evidence, it would seem of the feasibility of analyzing, by recourse to the present paradigm, systems that are not dominated by a "legislature." In the section of operationalizing concepts, however, a number of suggestions were made on how institutionalization might be measured with respect to executive structures and political parties. One could assume that if the cognate variables pertaining to executives or parties were substituted for those pertaining to the legislature for cases involving executive or party dominance of the law-making function, the results would be similar to those of the pilot study. Even though we should not have any substantial difficulties in measuring institutionalization in these other structures, we would still be faced with a serious dilemma if we attempted to compare in the same analysis executive-, party-, and legislature-dominated systems. The problem is that we could not assume the measurement scales for each of the three categories of systems would be comparable. Indeed, the variables employed as indicators of openness and rationality would be different for each of the three types of systems. After considerably more empirical investigation, it might eventually be possible to standardize scores across systems, but this hardly seems in the offing at the present.

Clearly, the way out of the dilemma is to tricotomize the analysis. Three models, representing executive, party, and legislature dominance, would have to be tested separately. This would, of course, preclude the making of generalizations across types of systems or the making of inferences about the total population of political systems. All inferences, in other words, would have to be specific to the type of system in terms of the institutions that dominated the legislative function. This may be considered an important limitation of the paradigm, but it is not a fatal flaw. Some meaningful comparisons can still be made between types of systems, such as which type tended to be the most responsive. Also, the possibility has been suggested that we should be able to develop standardized scales for measuring institutionalization which would apply across all types of systems once we know more about the pattern of relationships between the institutionalization and the other endogenous variables.

Thomas Kuhn (1970) has noted that the acceptance of a new paradigm in a scientific discipline generally depends on its being useful in solving some vexing scientific "puzzles" that the old paradigms were unable to solve or even to approach. The new paradigm presented here can at least approach, and can probably solve, the puzzle of how to evaluate political systems. Once this puzzle is solved, it then becomes possible to attack a number of other puzzles, such as, are the effects of institutionalization, and political and social differentiation beneficial or detrimental to the system? We cannot, on the basis of the pilot study, say that any of these puzzles is solved, but the study gave some indications of the promise of this approach. Although it also revealed some limitations and defects, the puzzle-solving potential of the paradigm seems high, and the fruitfulness of future work in this direction seems assured.

## NOTES

1. Pye (1962: 43), however, comments that "the whole range of modern political roles . . . have appeared in transitional societies not through response to the internal needs of the society itself, but in response to supranational and foreign concepts of the appropriate standards of modern governmental and political behavior." His statement may be true, but one would want to determine the stability, autonomy, and lack of interchangeability of these roles before one labeled these politically differentiated systems. It is doubtful that they would meet these tests.

2. In one respect this is not true because a number of the "newer" states do not have a history that is old enough to fit them into a very long longitudinal analysis. In the pilot study reported here, Alaska and Hawaii, which entered the Union in 1959, were excluded because of the short historical range of their statistics.

3. This was calculated from data from the U.S. Internal Revenue Service, *Individual Income Tax Returns* (various years). The number of returns with adjusted gross income of less than $3,000 was recorded. Then the total number of individuals 18 years and older not belonging to a family unit plus the number of family units was calculated from U.S. Census estimates in *Current Population Reports: Population Estimates*, Series P-25. This latter figure was regarded as an estimate of the maximum number of returns possible (if everyone had taxable income). From this figure, the total number of returns submitted from the state to the IRS was subtracted, which produced an estimate of the number of unattached individuals over 18 and family units without sufficient income to file a return (plus a few four-flushers). This difference was then added to the number of returns showing incomes of less than $3,000, which provided the final figure. A validation check was run on this by

correlating the estimate based on this method for 1960 with the number of unattached individuals and families with incomes of less than $3,000 as reported in the U.S. Census for 1960. The correlation was .93.

4. Measurement error is a particularly difficult problem with the need data used here. Except for 1960, all of these data are based on "intercensal" estimates, that is, they are data from the U.S. Census Bureau but are estimates based on interpolation, on small samples, or on multiple regression analysis.

5. I am indebted to Professor Weber of Indiana University who supplied me with the data for this index and with several other variables used in this study.

6. Using data relating to the overriding and sustaining of gubernatorial vetoes, McCally (1966) has devised one of the few behavioral indicators of gubernatorial legislative power. It is available, however, for less than half of the U.S. states.

7. This is the form for all of the interaction variables except those involving the legislative party competition index and the two party control variables. In the latter case the interaction is assumed to be multiplicative and therefore takes the form $(X_4)(X_3)$.

8. The actual analytical procedures employed a stepwise multiple regression program, which entered only those variables into the equation with regression coefficients having t-ratios greater than 2.0. As a consequence of this procedure, not all of the terms shown in equation 1 through 4 were necessarily present in the final regression equations.

9. Bell (1971) has even constructed a rather elaborate psychological explanation for the close association between political differentiation and turnover.

10. Had stepwise regression procedures not been used, and had all variables been included in the regression equation, then these four variables would, obviously, have been controlled in the sense that each coefficient in the equation represents the net effect of an independent variable with all other variables held constant. The very large number of variables in the model precluded that approach, however, because of the possibility of overdetermination of the dependent variable.

11. This dynamic procedure does not entirely eliminate the possibility of reciprocal causation, but it does rule out spuriousness such as that cited in the example where the prior condition of B could cause A as well as the later condition of B. With dynamic data, spuriousness could be created as an artifact of the measurement process. Suppose, for instance, that A actually caused B, could this be solely responsible for a correlation between changes in B and changes in A measured after the changes in B? This might be possible under one set of conditions. If A caused B, then everywhere that the value of A was large, the value of B would also tend to be large and where A was small, B would tend to be small. Further, if we were measuring change in terms of percentage increase or decrease, and the variables were of the sort that had upper limits, then as these were approached, percentage increases would tend to be less. This means that when A and B are both large, and they will tend to be both large together, measurement of percentage increase will tend to be minimal, whereas when they are both small percentage increases will tend to be greater. As a consequence, there could be a correlation between change in B measured prior to change in A and the latter and we would thereby tend to conclude that B caused A when the opposite was true.

# REFERENCES

BELL, R. (1971) "Notes for a theory of legislative behavior: the conceptual scheme," pp. 21-38 in H. Hirsch and M. D. Hancock (eds.) Comparative Legislative Systems. New York: The Free Press.

BINDER, L. et al. (1971) Crises and Sequence in Political Development. Princeton, N.J.: Princeton University Press.

Citizens Conference on State Legislatures (1971) State Legislatures: An Evaluation of Their Effectiveness. New York: Praeger.

COLEMAN, J. S. (1966) Equality of Educational Opportunity. Washington, D.C.: U.S. Office of Education.

DAVIT, P. T. and R. EISENBERG (1961) Devaluation of the Urban and Suburban Vote: A Statistical Investigation of Long-Term Trends in State Legislative Representation. Charlottesville: University of Virginia, Bureau of Public Administration.

DOWNS, A. (1967) Inside Bureaucracy. Boston: Little, Brown.

DUVERGER, M. (1951) Political Parties: Their Organization and Activity in the Modern State. London: Methuen.

EASTON, D. (1965) A Framework for Political Analysis. Englewood Cliffs, N.J.: Prentice-Hall.

ECKSTEIN, H. (1969) "Authority relations and governmental performance: a theoretical framework," Comparative Pol. Studies 2 (Oceober): 269-326.

EISENSTADT, S. N. (1964) Amer. Soc. Rev. 29 (April).

——— (1963) The Political System of Empires. New York: The Free Press.

ELDERSVELD, S. J. (1964) Political Parties: A Behavioral Analysis. Chicago: Rand McNally.

FRANCIS, W. (1968) Comparative Analysis of Legislative Issues in the Fifty States. New York: Rand McNally.

GRUMM, J. (1973) "The legislative system as an economic model," chap. 10 in A. Kornberg (ed.) Legislatures in Comparative Perspective. New York: David McKay.

GURR, T. R. (1968) "A causal model of civil strife: a comparative analysis using new indices." Amer. Pol. Sci. Rev. 62 (December): 1104-1124.

HOFFERBERT, R. I. (1966) "The relationships between public policy and some structural and environmental variables in the American states." American Political Science Review (January): 73-82

HOLT, R. T. and J. M. RICHARDSON, JR. (1970) "Competing paradigms in comparative politics," Chap. 2 in R. T. Holt and J. E. Turner (eds.) The Methodology of Comparative Research. New York: The Free Press.

——— and J. E. Turner (1970) The Methodology of Comparative Research. New York: The Free Press.

——— (1967) "A proposed structural-functional framework," in J. C. Charlesworth (ed.) Contemporary Political Analysis. New York: The Free Press.

HUNTINGTON, S. P. (1968) Political Order in Changing Societies. New Haven: Yale University Press.

JEWELL, M. E. and S. C. PATTERSON (1973) The Legislative Process in the United States. [2nd edn.] New York: Random House.

KATZ, E. and B. DANET (1973) Bureaucracy and the Public. New York: Basic Books.

KORNBERG, A. [ed.] (1973) Legislatures in Comparative Perspective. New York: David McKay.

— — —, H. D. CLARKE, and G. L. WATSON (1973a) "Toward a model of parliamentary recruitment in Canada," pp. 250-281 in A. Kornberg (ed.) Legislatures in Comparative Perspective. New York: David McKay.

KUHN, T. (1970) The Structure of Scientific Revolutions. Chicago: University of Chicago Press.

LASSWELL, H. D. (1963) The Future of Political Science. New York: Atherton.

LIEBERSON, S. (1969) "Measuring population diversity." Amer. Soc. Rev. 34 (December): 850-862.

LINDSAY, A. D. (1947) The Modern Democratic State, vol. 1. New York and London: Oxford University Press.

LOEWENBERG, G. (1972) "Comparative legislative research," chap. 1 in S. C. Patterson and J. C. Wahlke (eds.) Comparative Legislative Behavior: Frontiers of Research. New York: Wiley-Interscience.

McCALLY, S. P. (1966) "The governor and his legislative party." American Political Science Review 60 (December): 923-942.

PATTERSON, S. C., J. C. WAHLKE and G. R. BOYNTON (1973) "Dimensions of support in legislative systems," chap. 12 in A. Kornberg (ed.) Legislatures in Comparative Perspective. New York: David McKay.

— — — and M. E. JEWELL (1973) The Legislative Process in the United States. New York: Random House.

— — — and J. C. WAHLKE (1972) Comparative Legislative Behavior: Frontiers of Research. New York: Wiley-Interscience.

— — — (1971) "Political representation and public policy." Social Science Research Council Conference on the Impacts of Public Policy (unpublished).

POLSBY, N. W. (1968) "Institutionalization in the U.S. House of Representatives. American Political Science Review 62 (March): 144-168.

PYE, L. W. (1962) Personality, Politics, and Nation-Building: Burma's Search for Identity. New Haven: Yale University Press.

RIKER, W. H. (1962) The Theory of Political Coalitions. New Haven: Yale University Press.

SCHLESINGER, J. A. (1965) "The politics of the executive," chap. 6 in H. Jacob and K. N. Vines (eds.) Politics in the American States. Boston: Little, Brown.

SCHUBERT, G. A. and C. PRESS (1964) "Measuring and malapportionment." American Political Science Review 58 (June): 302-327.

SIMON, H. A. (1957) Administrative Behavior. New York: The Free Press.

SISSON, R. (1973) "Comparative legislative institutionalization: a theoretical exploration," chap. 1 in A. Kornberg (ed.) Legislatures in Comparative Perspective. New York: David McKay.

SULLIVAN, J. L. (1973) "Political correlates of social, economic, and religious diversity in the American states." Journal of Politics 35 (February): 70-84.

TULLOCK, G. (1965) The Politics of Bureaucracy. Washington: Public Affairs Press.

WAHLKE, J. C. et. al. (1962) The Legislative System. New York: John Wiley.

WEBER, R. E. and W. P. SHAFFER (1970) "The State public policy-making process, political culture, and public opinion: a limited consideration of a general model." Meeting of the Midwest Political Science Association (unpublished).

JOHN G. GRUMM is Professor of Political Science at Wesleyan University. Previously, he has taught at the University of Kansas and at the University of California at Berkeley. He has served as Research Director of the Citizen's Conference on State Legislatures. As Staff Director of the Federal Advisory Committee on Higher Education, as a special legislative assistant to Governor Edmund G. Brown of California, and has been Book Review Editor of the Midwest Journal of Political Science. The results of his research in the fields of legislative studies and state government have been published in professional journals and as contributions to books.